Time to Talk

Time to Talk provides a powerful and accessible resource for practitioners to help develop their own skills, as well as supporting a whole-school or setting approach to speaking and listening. Written by the government's former Communication Champion for children, it showcases and celebrates effective approaches in schools and settings across the country. Jean Gross helpfully summarises research on what helps children and young people develop good language and communication skills, and highlights the importance of key factors: a place to talk, a reason to talk and support for talk.

This practical, engaging and full colour book also provides:

- whole-class approaches to developing all children and young people's speaking and listening skills;
- 'catch-up' strategies for those with limited language;
- ways in which settings and schools can develop an effective partnership with specialists (such as speech and language therapists) to help children with more severe needs;
- examples of good practice in supporting parents/carers to develop their children's language skills; and
- answers to practitioners' most frequently asked questions about speech and language.

This book is for all school leaders, teachers and early-years practitioners concerned about the growing number of children and young people with limited language and communication skills.

Jean Gross CBE has recently been England's Communication Champion for children, responsible for promoting the importance of good language skills for all children and young people, and improving services for those needing help in learning to communicate. She is the author of numerous articles and best-selling books on children's issues, including *Beating Bureaucracy in Special Educational Needs* (2nd edition, David Fulton).

nasen is a professional membership association that supports all those who work with or care for children and young people with special and additional educational needs. Members include teachers, teaching assistants, support workers, other educationalists, students and parents.

nasen supports its members through policy documents, journals, its magazine Special!, publications, professional development courses, regional networks and newsletters. Its website contains more current information such as responses to government consultations. **nasen's** published documents are held in very high regard both in the UK and internationally.

Other titles published in association with the National Association for Special Educational Needs (nasen):

Brilliant Ideas for Using ICT in the Inclusive Classroom
Sally McKeown and Angela McGlashon
2011/pb: 978-0-415-67254-2

Language for Learning in the Secondary School: A Practical Guide for Supporting Students with Speech, Language and Communication Needs
Sue Hayden and Emma Jordan
2012/pb: 978-0-415-61975-2

ADHD: All Your Questions Answered: A Complete Handbook for SENCOs and Teachers
Fintan O'Regan
2012/pb: 978-0-415-59770-8

Assessing Children with Specific Learning Difficulties: A Teacher's Practical Guide
Gavin Reid, Gad Elbeheri and John Everatt
2012/pb: 978-0-415-67027-2

Time to Talk

Implementing outstanding practice in speech, language and communication

Jean Gross

Taylor & Francis Group

LONDON AND NEW YORK

Helping Everyone Achieve

First published 2013
by Routledge
2 Park Square, Milton Park, Abingdon, Oxon OX14 4RN

Simultaneously published in the USA and Canada
by Routledge
711 Third Avenue, New York, NY 10017

Routledge is an imprint of the Taylor & Francis Group, an informa business

British Library Cataloguing in Publication Data
A catalogue record for this book is available from the British Library

Library of Congress Cataloging in Publication Data
Library of Congress Cataloging-in-Publication Data
Gross, Jean.
Time to talk : implementing outstanding practice in speech, language and
communication / Authored by Jean Gross.
pages cm
Includes index.
1. Language arts (Elementary)–Great Britain. 2. Literacy programs–Great Britain.
3. Mainstreaming in education–Great Britain. 4. Communication–Education. I. Title.
LB1576.G785 2013
372.6–dc23
2012048238

ISBN: 978-0-415-63333-8 (hbk)
ISBN: 978-0-415-63334-5 (pbk)
ISBN: 978-0-203-09510-2 (ebk)

Typeset in Bembo
by FiSH Books Ltd, Enfield

Printed and bound in India by Replika Press Pvt. Ltd.

Contents

Preface

For the two years between 2010 and 2012, I had the privilege of being the government's Communication Champion, charged with raising awareness of the importance of good communication skills for children and young people, and identifying and disseminating examples of good practice. One of my roles was to work with the Communication Trust to lead a national year of communication – the 2011 Hello campaign.

During those two years I travelled the country and saw many examples of inspiring practice in early years settings, schools, local authorities and their partner health services. Many people also contacted me to tell me about their work. I became, for a while, a kind of repository of good ideas about developing language and communication skills for all children and young people, and providing effective help for those who struggle in this area.

It is these ideas I want to pass on through this book. I am deeply grateful to all who shared their practice so generously; I hope I have acknowledged their work. I also know, however, that from time to time I may unwittingly have drawn on ideas whose source I have been unable to trace. If so, please let me know and I will make sure that your work is appropriately credited in any future editions.

Particular thanks go to all at the Communication Trust, ICAN and the National Literacy Trust for their expertise, and to Nasen for all their help during the national year of communication and their support for this publication. I am also very grateful to all the brilliant speech and language therapists who taught me so much about language, to all the settings and schools who feature as case studies in this book, and to those who helped me source photographs of communication-supportive environments: Elizabeth Jarman, Carol-Ann Howe and schools in North Yorkshire, Torriano Junior School in Camden, the speech and language therapy service and Foley Park Primary School in Worcestershire, the speech and language therapy service and schools in Lewisham, Lancasterian Specialist School in Manchester, schools and support services in Rochdale, and staff at Derwentwater Primary School in Ealing. Finally, big thanks go to Esme, Reuben, Oscar and Isaac (and their parents) for donating their lovely photos for use in this book.

Jean Gross CBE
October 2012

Speech, language and communication – a growing issue

A growing issue

The ability to communicate – to say what you want to say and to understand what other people are saying – is fundamental to life chances.

Some of the statistics about the links between language skills and life chances are startling. For example:

- vocabulary at age five is one of the most significant predictors of the qualifications pupils achieve when they leave school;
- more than half of children starting school in socially disadvantaged areas of England have delayed language; and
- two thirds of 7- to 14-year-olds with serious behaviour problems have language impairment.

Numbers of children and young people with difficulties in language appear to be growing. During the five years between 2005 and 2010, government figures show a 58 per cent rise in those with speech, language and communication needs as their primary type of special educational need (SEN).

Head teachers are also increasingly concerned about the numbers of pupils starting school with limited language skills – using a very restricted vocabulary and not talking in sentences. This is often linked to social deprivation, but not exclusively so. In my time as Communication Champion I met many teachers in affluent areas who told me about children of 'cash-rich, time-poor' parents who were starting school unable to hold a conversation. One such child had recently been bought a BlackBerry by his parents.

There is much speculation about the reasons for poor communication skills, from over-use of technology, or less time for parents to talk with their children, to the invention of central heating (which means families don't have to be in one room any more in order to keep warm). We have little hard evidence one way or another to prove whether these social changes are causing a rise in language difficulties, but the end result is a problem that schools and settings increasingly feel the need to address.

Talk in the classroom

There is much research evidence that children achieve better where their classrooms provide rich opportunities for talk. The Cambridge Primary Review (Alexander, 2009) undertook an extensive review of the literature and concluded that we should 'Make a concerted effort to ensure that language, particularly spoken language, achieves its full potential as a key to cognitive development, learning and successful teaching.'

The influential EPPSI study (Siraj-Blatchford *et al.*, 2011) found that teachers in highly effective schools used dialogic teaching and learning, involving collaborative talk and instructional conversations. Similarly, a number of Ofsted thematic national reports have identified effective practice in speaking and listening as a key feature of outstanding schools.

Extracts from national Ofsted reports

In the most effective schools visited, inspectors saw teachers thread rich opportunities for speaking and listening into lessons. In turn, this led to improved standards in writing.
– Ofsted Annual Report 2009/10

A common feature of the most successful schools in the survey was the attention they gave to developing speaking and listening.
– Removing Barriers to Literacy, January 2011

In the schools visited, there were 'opportunities for developing mathematical language so that pupils learned to express their thinking using the correct vocabulary'.
– Good Practice in Primary Mathematics: Evidence from 20 Successful Schools, November 2011

Current policies

Perhaps because of this evidence about the importance of talk, current national policy is beginning to place a much greater emphasis on oral language than it did in the previous two decades.

The revised Early Years Foundation Stage curriculum gives a high priority to language and communication as one of three prime areas of learning. No longer is it part of literacy; it is there in its own right. Government have also noted, in their vision for the Foundation Years (DfE, 2011), that they intend to 'drive improvements in the quality of free early education, promoting a strong emphasis on speech, language and communication as central to good provision.'

At the time of writing, we await the revised National Curriculum for 5- to 19-year-olds, but it is likely also to prioritise oral language. The 2012 professional standards for teachers include a requirement that all teachers, whatever subject they teach, must be able to promote 'articulacy' as well as literacy.

Finally, Ofsted have included in the 2012 inspection framework for schools (Ofsted, 2012) the extent to which:

- pupils develop a range of skills, including reading, writing, communication and mathematical skills, and how well they apply these across the curriculum; and
- reading, writing, communication and mathematics are well taught.

Are we ready?

For all the reasons above, language and communication is a 'hot topic' for all those who work in education. There is a long way to go, however, in changing practice. For many schools and settings spoken language has for too long taken a back seat. I will never forget, for example, the maths teacher who was interviewed for a survey on attitudes to spoken language in the curriculum and said 'Communication is not important in my lesson.' This is an extreme example, but I would invite you to reflect on the diagram in Table 1.1, which suggests that while listening and speaking are learned first in infancy and childhood, and used most throughout both childhood and adult life, they are taught least in our schools. Does the diagram apply to your school or to the schools you work with?

Table 1.1 Learned, used, taught

	Listening	**Speaking**	**Reading**	**Writing**
Learned	first	second	third	third
Used	most	next to most	next to least	least
Taught	least	next to least	next to most	most

Turning the dial

Schools that 'turn the dial' on language and communication are able to turn the dial on a number of key school improvement priorities, from raising attainment to narrowing the gap and improving behaviour.

Attainment

Good speech and language skills predict school attainment. As head teachers know, the barrier for many children in achieving Level 4+ in English at the end of Key Stage 2 is their lack of oral language to support reading comprehension and writing.

- Vocabulary at age five is a very strong predictor of the qualifications achieved at school leaving age and beyond (Feinstein and Duckworth, 2006).
- Early speech, language and communication difficulties are a very significant predictor of later literacy difficulties (Snowling, 2006).
- At the age of six there is a gap of a few months between the reading age of children who had good oral language skills at five, and those who had poor oral language skills at five. By the time they are 14, this gap has widened to *five years'* difference in reading age (Hirsch, 1996).

- Research in one local authority found that children achieving below Level 2 in Reading and Writing at the end of KS1 had an average standardised score of only 75 on a test of oral language skills – 11 points less than those who achieved Level 2+. There was no difference between the groups on non-verbal intelligence. At KS2 there was an even bigger gap – of 19 points – between the language skills of those who achieved Level 4+ in English and those who didn't (Gross, 2002).

Narrowing the gap

Many schools are finding that a strategy to address children's impoverished language is playing a key part in their efforts to narrow the attainment gap between less well-off children and their peers.

Language skills are a critical factor in social disadvantage:

- On average a toddler from a family on welfare will hear around 600 words per hour, with a ratio of two prohibitions ('stop that', 'get down off there') to one encouraging comment. A child from a professional family will hear over 2000 words per hour, with a ratio of six encouraging comments to one negative (Hart and Risley, 2003).
- While, as we have seen, language difficulties are not confined to socially disadvantaged areas, Jane Waldfogel (using data from a large cohort of children born in the year 2000) found an average 16-month gap in vocabulary between children from the most and least wealthy families, at the age of five. The gap in language was very much larger than gaps in other cognitive skills (Waldfogel and Washbrook, 2010).
- More than half of children starting nursery school in socially disadvantaged areas of England have delayed language. While their general cognitive abilities are in the average range for their age, their language skills are well behind (Locke et al., 2002)
- Vocabulary at age five has been found to be the best predictor (from a range of measures at age five and ten) of whether children who experienced social deprivation in childhood were able to 'buck the trend' and escape poverty in later adult life (Blanden, 2006).
- Research has shown that gaps in language ability between more and less disadvantaged children persist in to secondary school. One study (Spencer et al., 2012), for example, found significant differences between the scores of pupils living in disadvantaged areas when compared to more affluent areas on comprehension of spoken paragraphs, sentence length and vocabulary. They did not differ on a measure of non-verbal ability. 21 per cent of the pupils in the socially disadvantaged cohort had clinically significant and hitherto undetected language difficulties.

Behaviour and wellbeing

Speech and language skills also predict behaviour and wellbeing. Good language skills act as a 'protective factor' which reduces the likelihood of poor school attendance, truancy, delinquency and substance misuse.

- Two-thirds of 7- to 14-year-olds with serious behaviour problems have language impairment (Cohen et al. 1998).
- Two thirds of young offenders have speech, language and communication difficulties, but in only 5 per cent of cases were they identified before the offending began (Bryan, 2008).

Employability

The changing jobs market means that spoken communication skills, along with influencing skills, computing skills and literacy skills, have shown the greatest increase in employer-rated importance over the last 10 years (UK Commission for Employment and Skills, 2010).

- 47 per cent of employers in England report difficulty in finding employees with an appropriate level of oral communication skills (UK Commission for Employment and Skills, 2010).
- Language difficulties have been identified as a key risk factor in becoming NEET – that is, 'not in employment, education or training' (Scottish Social Research Executive, 2005).
- In one study, 88 per cent of young unemployed men were found to have language difficulties (Elliott, 2009).

These are just some of the many reasons why school and early years setting leadership teams might see speech, language and communication needs as crucial to their setting or school improvement planning.

The scale of the problem

School census data shows that speech, language and communication needs (SLCN) are the most common type of primary SEN in primary schools, making up 29 per cent of the total (DfE, 2012).

As we have seen, some theorists believe that growing numbers reflect a growing social problem, with links to disadvantage. But it is not just a social problem. Irrespective of disadvantage, and irrespective of wider societal factors like time spent on TV and texting and computer games, international research shows that around 7 per cent of children have a biologically based specific language impairment that makes it difficult for them to process language.

On top of this, we have another 3 per cent who have SLCN linked to another type of need, such as hearing or physical impairment, Down syndrome or autism. So that makes at least 10 per cent – on average, three children per reception class – who need extra help with speech, language or communication. And then we have the equally significant (though actually easier to remedy) language delays linked to social disadvantage.

So the sheer scale of SLCN is one reason for making sure that it is part of schools' or settings' planning to improve outcomes for children.

Children learning English as an additional language

Another reason for focusing on spoken communication a key strategy for school improvement is the increasing numbers of pupils in our schools who are learning English as an additional language (EAL). EAL learners now make up over one in seven of the school population.

To be an EAL learner is not of itself a problem or a deficit – the opposite, in fact, since research is showing that EAL learners have superior problem-solving skills, and 'executive function' ability to filter and focus on information that is important (Lauchlan *et al.*, 2012), perhaps because of the mental alertness they develop in order to switch between languages. But it does mean that the child has a need for additional support in acquiring English, in order to succeed academically.

This need may not always be obvious. The well-known theorist Professor Jim Cummins (Cummins, 2008) makes the distinction between two differing kinds of language proficiency

– 'BICS' and 'CALP'. BICS are basic interpersonal communication skills; these are the 'surface' skills of listening and speaking that are typically acquired quickly by many students, particularly by those from language backgrounds similar to English who spend a lot of their school time interacting with native speakers.

CALP is cognitive academic language proficiency, and, as the name suggests, is the basis for a child's ability to cope with the academic demands placed on them across the school curriculum. CALP tends to have a high degree of context independence or 'disembedding', and a high incidence of low-frequency vocabulary and grammatical complexity (for example, the use of subordinate clauses, and of nominalisation – where verbs and adjectives expressing concrete ideas are turned into abstract nouns, so that 'how quickly cracks in glass grow' becomes 'glass crack growth rate').

Cummins notes that while many second language learners develop conversational fluency (BICS) within two years of immersion in the target language, it takes much longer (five to seven years) to learn the more academic language (CALP).

Cummins has another very helpful model, which describes the task of teachers in working with EAL learners. The model (Figure 1.1) categorises different learning tasks along two dimensions. One dimension reflects the level of cognitive challenge in the task, ranging from cognitively undemanding to cognitively demanding. The other dimension reflects the degree of contextual support, from context-embedded to context-reduced. A context-embedded task is one in which the student has access to a range of additional visual and oral cues; for example, they can look at illustrations of what is being talked about or ask questions to confirm understanding. A context-reduced task is one such as listening to a lecture or reading dense text, where there are no sources of help other than the language itself. Clearly, a D quadrant task, which is both cognitively demanding and context-reduced, is likely to be the most difficult for students, particularly for non-native speakers in their first years of learning English. However, it is essential that EAL students develop the ability to accomplish such tasks, since academic success is impossible without it.

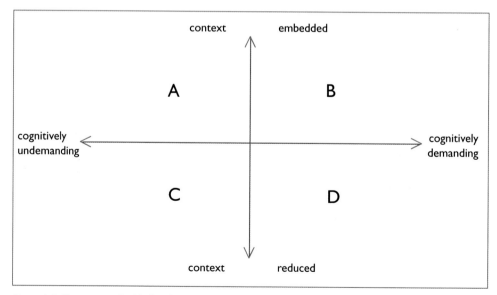

Figure 1.1 Context-embedded and context-reduced tasks

One of the lightbulb moments for me in my time as Communication Champion was the realisation that this model does not only apply to EAL learners. It also applies to children whose environment has not provided them with opportunities to hear and use context-reduced language. It applies to children who have not had stories told to them, or had opportunities to engage in sophisticated conversations at home that are about events and ideas beyond the immediate here and now.

So the task for school improvement seems to me to move children from everyday conversational language to disembedded formal talk – talk which, unlike informal conversational talk, does not depend on seeing what is happening for comprehension – *whatever* the reason for the child's need for help in making to make that crucial transition.

Yet this is difficult for schools. There is an intriguing historic lack of interface between the understandings of two different 'camps' – the experts who deal with EAL and those who deal with children with special needs in speech, language and communication. It is clear, however, that graphic organisers from the EAL world can support children with SLCN, that visual timetables and Widgit symbols beloved of the SEN/SLCN world can support EAL learners, and that the progression in language structures for EAL learners (which I will describe in Chapter 6) is in fact a progression that can apply to all children.

I hope this book will help to bridge these different sources of expertise.

Can we make a difference?

No studies so far have directly followed up the later impact of interventions to improve children and young people's language skills on end of key stage attainment or employability. We know, however, that:

- Children whose language difficulties were resolved by the age of five and a half were more likely to go on to develop good reading and spelling skills – and keep pace with their peers, passing as many exams on leaving school as children without a history of language disorder (Conti-Ramsden et al., 2009).
- Key Stage 2 children with poor reading comprehension made greater improvements in reading when provided with an intervention to develop their oral language than they did when provided with an intervention directly targeting reading comprehension skills (Snowling et al., 2010).
- Socially disadvantaged children can catch up with other children in language skills after just nine months if their teachers are trained to have the right kind of conversations with them (Hank and Deacon, 2008).
- Small group interventions to boost language skills have a rapid, measurable effect on vocabulary and other aspects of language development – themselves very strong predictors of later academic achievement. Key Stage 1 children receiving one such intervention, for example, made on average eighteen months progress on a test of vocabulary and language development after just ten weeks of group help (Lee, 2011).
- It is never too late. Re-conviction rates for offenders who studied the English Speaking Board's oral communication course fell to 21 per cent (compared with the national average of 44 per cent), greater than the fall to 28 per cent for offenders who followed a general education course (Moseley et al., 2006).

The impact of national initiatives

The national Every Child a Talker initiative provides evidence of the impact that is possible when concerted action is taken to target language and communication skills. Every Child a Talker was implemented between 2008 and 2011, eventually reaching all local authority areas in England. It provided professional development for early-years practitioners to develop their own skills and enable them to increase the involvement of parents in supporting children's language in the home. In Every Child a Talker each local area involved was funded for an Early Language Consultant (a post often shared between a speech and language therapist and a teacher). Settings involved all assessed children's language development using a child monitoring profiling tool, which identifies children who are not at age-expected levels in the four strands of attention and listening, speaking, understanding and social communication. Where children were identified as delayed, staff provided targeted support.

Robust national and local impact data were generated from the programme's child monitoring profiling tool. Among the 114,000 children involved there was a reduction of between 10 and 14 per cent in the number of children showing language delay across all four strands, and large increases in the percentage of children performing ahead of age-related expectations. Figures 1.2 and 1.3 show the data for the first 'wave' of local authorities involved.

National data from the Early Years Foundation Stage Profile also suggest a significant impact for Every Child a Talker. Over the 2007–2010 period, there was an overall ten per cent increase in the numbers of children achieving a good level of development on the profile's 'Language for Communication and Thinking' scale. Interestingly, between 2010 and 2011, when Every Child a Talker was reaching its peak numbers of children, there was also a reduction from 4 to 3 per cent in the percentage of five-year-olds showing very significant difficulties on this scale.

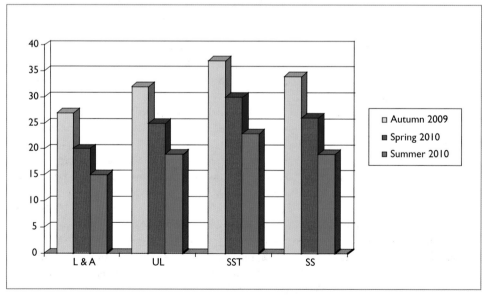

Figure 1.2 Every Child a Talker national data: percentage of children showing language delay

Notes: L&A: listening and attention; UL: understanding language; SST: speech sounds and talk; SS: social skills

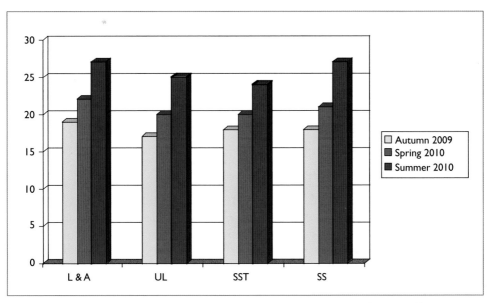

Figure 1.3 Every Child a Talker national data: percentage of children ahead of expected language development levels

Notes: L&A: listening and attention; UL: understanding language; SST: speech sounds and talk; SS: social skills

The case study below illustrates the impact of Every Child a Talker in one local authority.

CASE STUDY

In Bolton, a speech and language therapist and an early years consultant (a member of the inclusion support teaching service) supported twenty settings, providing a well-regarded model of training (Elklan; see www.elklan.co.uk) to Early Language Lead Professionals, who ranged from assistant head teachers to foundation phase leads to nursery practitioners and heads of 'rooms' in settings. Training also included Elizabeth Jarman's influential Communication Friendly Spaces™ and Bags for Families approaches. Each setting was also offered time from the speech and language therapist or consultant to model the running of small group 'Nursery Narrative' programme two or three times a week for twenty minutes a time. All children were assessed before and after this intervention using a standardised language measure in addition to the Every Child a Talker child monitoring profiling tool.

After two terms, children made an average 26 point gain when the normal expectation would be a three point gain. There were also very significant reductions in the numbers of children behind age norms in the 1200 children involved; between January and June, numbers showing delay showed a drop of between 15 and 26 percentage points across the four monitoring profile tool strands. Put another way, this meant that *the equivalent of ten whole reception classes were no longer showing delay*.

The work is now being extended into further schools, and up the age range, with a target of 40 per cent of schools being involved and an aim that every setting and school will have its own Communication Champion.

Moving down the age range, the local authority used the principles of Every Child a Talker in their provision of free daycare provision for two-year-olds in socially deprived areas. Children were screened using a Healthy Child Programme checklist, and their settings were supported with targeted training in speech and language.

The impact of local strategic action

Other evidence to show that it is possible to make a difference to language and communication development comes from local areas like Stoke-on-Trent, Sheffield and Nottinghamshire, which have recognised children and young people's communication skills as a priority, and developed community-wide, interagency strategies to upskill the children's workforce and get key messages across to parents. Strategies like these can make a significant difference. The 'Stoke Speaks Out' early-years campaign has succeeded in reducing the percentage of three- to four-year-olds with language delay from 64 per cent in 2004 to 39 per cent in 2010. Sheffield's 'Every Sheffield Child Articulate and Literate by 11' initiative witnessed an improvement of seven percentage points in the proportion of five year old children achieving a good level of development in communication, language and literacy and personal, social and emotional development in the first year of implementing the strategy, and a significant closing of the gap between the lowest-achieving children and their peers. The percentage of children in Sheffield achieving above the expected level in reading and in writing at age seven also increased markedly, underpinned by schools' focus on speaking and listening. There was a nine per cent increase in the number of schools receiving good or outstanding Ofsted judgements for pupils' achievement and the extent to which they enjoy their learning, and for pupils' behaviour.

CASE STUDY

Stoke Speaks Out is a multi-agency strategy set up in 2004 to tackle the high incidence of speech and language difficulties in Stoke-on-Trent. It aims to support attachment, parenting and speech and language issues through training, support and advice. It developed from local Sure Start initiatives, which identified that between 60 and 80 per cent of children assessed in Stoke at age three to four years had a language delay.

A common early years assessment tool is now used by all agencies from health visitors to early years consultants to speech and language therapists. Practitioners in early years settings are trained to know whether a child's language and social development is age-appropriate. Following an audit of skills that showed that health visitors had had no training in child development, all members of the health visiting team receive a two-day child development module that covers essential skills parents need to help their child build the basics for learning.

The programme has developed a multi-agency training framework for all practitioners working in the city with children from birth to seven years, or their families. The training has five levels, ranging from awareness-raising to detailed theoretical levels, and was jointly written by the project team of speech and language therapists, a psychologist, a midwife, play workers, teachers and a bilingual worker. All levels have an expectation that the practitioner will create change in their working environment. In addition the initiative has developed resources for parents, including a model for toddler groups to follow which enhances language development, and a website offering practical information for parents to help with children's language development. 'Talking walk-ins' provide drop in sessions at Children's Centres where parents can get advice from speech and language therapists.

CASE STUDY

'Every Sheffield Child Articulate and Literate' (ESCAL) is a city-wide strategy delivering a systematic, lively approach to the development of communication skills from birth to age 11. Interest from secondary schools means that it is now beginning to expand to age 19. ESCAL brings together partners in the local authority learning and achievement service, the speech and language therapy service, health visitors, midwives, universities, housing, services for looked after children, libraries and museums.

The strategy aims to ensure that:

- every child is listened to and is able to express themselves confidently;
- children with delayed or impaired speech, language and communication receive support;
- practitioners know how to develop communication skills across a broad curriculum and how to track progress; and
- parents/carers are involved at all stages.

ESCAL uses the 'three-Wave' model:

- Wave 1 (Universal): Leadership development, universal multi-agency training for all early-years and primary practitioners, a speech and language tracking tool from birth to age 11, a consistent approach to visual support, an audit tool for communication-friendly schools, strategies to promote communication across the curriculum, parental involvement resources and parents' accreditation.
- Wave 2 (Targeted): Intervention packages (language enrichment, vocabulary development and narrative skills) and a Talk Volunteer programme.
- Wave 3 (Specialist Services): A 'team around the child' approach, with specialist training, and workshops delivered by speech and language therapists to parents of children with language impairment.

Agencies work together to promote a high profile for talk. Schools have been provided, for example, with wooden soapboxes for children to use to develop their speaking and listening skills, culminating in a 'Speakers' Corner' event. A Mad Hatters Talk Picnic took place in the city centre, involving over 1000 children. Key messages reached over 100,000 local people through media coverage of this event. Creative and cultural industries provided events such as Voice Explosion (Sheffield Theatres), Talking Movies (Cineworld) and Big Broadcasting Podcasting (Hallam FM radio).

There has been a major focus on reaching disadvantaged or hard-to-reach communities, including a Family Time marketing campaign and Family Time Workshops about supporting children's language in the home, delivered in targeted areas of the city. A top-tips poster for new parents was put on display in the hospital maternity wing, distributed by health visitors and published in the local paper, reaching 40,000 readers. A partnership with the Child Poverty Strategy enabled the Family Time campaign to run with teen and lone parents and the Yemeni/Somali community. Family Learning activities (Talking Together and Family Chatter Bags) have been provided in targeted areas. Speech and language therapy is now provided in schools, reducing the number of families not accessing services.

Local community strategies

As well as high-impact strategies to improve children's communication across a whole local authority area, we are beginning to see a growth in more local strategies, which take a 'cradle to college' approach across a community. One example is the 'Talk of the Town' initiative, in the Wythenshawe area of Manchester.

CASE STUDY

In the 'Talk of the Town' initiative, The Communication Trust worked with a secondary school, its feeder primaries, Children's Centres and multi-agency partners in one area of Manchester. The project aimed to embed the early identification of language and communication difficulties and a continuum of effective support.

The needs in this socially disadvantaged area are great. Assessment at the start of the initiative showed that more than a quarter of three- to four-year-olds in the schools' nursery classes had standardised scores below 70 – that is, at a level that would meet the criteria for a statement of special educational needs in many local authorities. 27 per cent of a random sample of children in Key Stage 1 tested at this 'severely delayed' level, compared with 2.7 per cent of children nationally. There was a similar picture in Key Stage 2, with poor vocabulary emerging as a particular issue. Half the children tested had significant difficulties on a naming task. At secondary level the incidence of difficulties was even higher; a staggering 50 per cent of the random sample of thirteen-year-olds assessed fell into the level that would meet statementing criteria.

Activities undertaken by the federation of schools included:

- employing a speech and language therapist seconded from the local service, to work in a consultative way with staff;
- allocating responsibility for communication and language to senior members of staff;
- building links with children's centres, so as to provide universal and targeted support to parents of young children in the area;

- putting in place permanent systems to assess all children and young people's language development, and track their progress over time;
- providing additional small group interventions delivered by trained teaching assistants;
- undertaking audits of the extent to which school and setting environments were communication-friendly;
- implementing classroom work to develop children and young people's listening skills and vocabulary; and
- enabling staff across the settings involved to undertake training on speech, language and communication, including a specific Level 3 award.

The impact of the initiative has been remarkable. Reassessments undertaken by an independent specialist show substantial increases in standardised scores on a range of language tests after just one year. Both the primary schools involved have improved in Ofsted inspections, achieving 'good with outstanding features' grades. External evaluation by the University of Manchester (Ainscow *et al.*, 2012) concluded that Talk of the Town has led to significant changes in thinking and practices, commending the project as a powerful approach for improving speech, language and communication among children and young people from disadvantaged backgrounds, and noting that 'this in turn offers encouraging possibilities for improving educational outcomes more generally, and in the longer term, the life chances of young people'.

Summary

In this chapter we have looked at why children and young people's language and communication development matters, and examined the multiple reasons for making it a setting and school improvement priority. We have also considered the evidence that shows we can make a difference. We do not have to simply bemoan children's declining language skills; we can take action to improve them, and see results.

The action we take, however, needs to be underpinned by an understanding of research and theory. We need to know how language develops, and how the environments we provide at home, in settings and in schools can best support that development. This is the theme of the next chapter.

What do we know about how to support language development?

Language represents how we think and is the medium for learning. It is also what makes us uniquely human. We come into life hard-wired to learn very quickly from the language we hear around us. Even in the womb, a baby can distinguish speech sounds from non-speech sounds. Soon after birth it will recognise its mother's voice. Children learn to use as many as 13,000 different words by the time they are six, and this vocabulary will grow to around 60,000 for a college student.

But not all children and young people follow this path. Learning language is complex, so much so that no one has yet been able to programme a computer to do what we as human beings seem to do 'by magic'. For some learners, the complexity of language acquisition presents real obstacles.

In this chapter we look at what research can tell us about language acquisition, and the factors which support it.

The language development pyramid

In my time as Communication Champion I came across several important pieces of information that helped me understand the process of language acquisition better.

One was a simple diagram: the language development pyramid widely used by speech and language therapists (Figure 2.1). The diagram is helpful because it reminds us that what we often see as 'language' (the speech that comes out of a child's mouth) is actually only a small part of a bigger picture. More important are the building blocks that underpin speech.

First of these is the ability to attend and listen to others, so that the child has input from which they can learn. Second comes the capacity for play and interaction, which provides the fundamental context in which language is learned. From these building blocks develops children's understanding of language (sometimes called receptive language), then their ability to express themselves through talk (their vocabulary and sentence structures).

What this means is that practitioners working with children and young people of all ages should not over-focus, as often happens now, on the clarity of the child's speech – their ability to manipulate speech sounds. More important questions to ask ourselves may be whether and how far the child is able to listen and attend, to play and interact, to understand what we say to them, and to express themselves with an age-appropriate vocabulary and language structure.

If, for example, we find that they have difficulty in listening and attending, that may be the place to begin any support or intervention. In an early years setting, we might notice that a child or group of children tend to flit from one thing to another with only a momentary focus on an activity. We could start by creating an enticing small space with a few objects inside that

Figure 2.1 The language development pyramid

really interest them, so as to encourage them to focus. In a primary or secondary classroom, we might explicitly teach and practise the skills of listening.

If we find that children can focus but interact little with adults or other children, we might in an early years setting start by getting down to their level, and simply watching and commenting on their play. In a primary school we might work with a whole class on how to strike up and sustain a conversation with a visitor to the school. In a secondary school we might provide a social skills group.

If we find that children are not understanding well the language that they hear, it will be an absolute priority to tackle this by teaching the vocabulary they do not understand, adjusting the complexity of the language we use with them, and so on. They will not be able to develop their own use of language (talking) unless we also work on their comprehension.

You will find strategies for addressing all the building blocks of the language development pyramid in the chapters that follow.

Three elements of language

Another important and linked concept used by speech and language therapists, but also with huge implications for education, is that there are three broad and different elements of language:

- **Receptive language**: what we understand from the language of others.
- **Expressive language**: how we talk with others through increasingly sophisticated language structures and expanded vocabulary.
- **Pragmatic language**: how we interact and have conversations with others, using and understanding the subtleties of facial expressions, body movements, tone, volume, inflection, ideas about when to speak and for how long, ideas about what the other person might want to know, and the ability to adopt different styles and conventions according to who we are talking to or with.

What this means for all those concerned with children and young people's language development is that there is a need to focus learning opportunities on all of these three elements. For example, it may be just as important to work with a group of teenagers on when and how to switch between street talk and formal talk as it is to develop their grammar. It will be just as important for a parent or early-years practitioner to read stories using rich patterns of intonation in their voices as it is to point out the names of characters or objects in the book.

What really matters in early language development

The next important information I want to share here comes from a literature review on the factors which support language acquisition, undertaken by the University of Dundee. This report (National Literacy Trust, 2010) focuses on birth to three years of age, but research with older children suggests that many of the key factors identified apply across the age range. These key factors are:

- the amount of language spoken to a child;
- the extent to which adults cue in and respond sensitively to what a child is trying to communicate;
- the way adults talk with children;
- reminiscing about events;
- sharing rhymes, songs and books;
- avoiding background noise;
- opportunities for interaction with other children; and
- continued use of the home language when children are growling up bilingual.

Let us look at each of these in turn.

Amount of language spoken to child

The sheer amount of language children hear is an important factor in their language development. Research shows that children with advanced language skills have parents who talk more, that talkative parents have talkative children, and that the earlier parents talk to their children (that is, as small babies) the better will be their later language ability.

There is more to this, however, than just the volume of words used. Researchers have found that the number of different word *types* used by parents is a key factor (Pan *et al.*, 2005). Complexity and breadth of vocabulary heard at home was found to make a significant difference to a child's language development by three, and their literacy development later on.

The extent to which adults cue in and respond sensitively to what a child is trying to communicate

Researchers have come up with a lovely metaphor to convey the optimal conditions for language development. The metaphor is based on tennis – 'serve and return'. The idea is that from birth, babies and children reach out for interaction, first through babbling, facial expressions and gestures, later by pointing at things to draw the adult's attention to them, later with speech. They 'serve'; the adult must return their serve by responding sensitively to what the baby or child is trying to communicate. If the baby or child does not get a response, or the response is inappropriate, then the brain's architecture does not form as it should. The child may also begin to 'serve' less, reducing their spontaneous communication. This is a pattern affecting practitioners working with children entering nursery or school, who may be quiet and not interact with adults or other children because they have ceased to expect a response.

To begin with, this sensitive, 'attuned' response to the child's comes from parents and carers. They in turn are biologically primed to be responsive communication partners, because of the strong emotional bond they have with the child. The psychologist Urie Bronfenbrenner has put this perfectly:

> In order to develop normally, a child requires progressively more complex joint activity with one or more adults who have an irrational emotional relationship with the child. Somebody's got to be crazy about that kid. That's number one. First, last and always.
>
> (Bronfenbrenner, 1994)

Taking part in conversational turns – the 'serve and return' – does not just apply to parents, however. As we will see later in this chapter, the extent to which practitioners in pre-school and school settings make time to listen to a child, tune in sensitively to what they are communicating and respond in kind will also have a profound effect on the child's language development.

Taking time to interact can be difficult in busy settings. Research cited in the Bercow review (Bercow, 2008), for example, found that only 40 per cent of children's time in early years settings was spent in interaction with other adults and children. In school classrooms, as we will see later in this book, the opportunities for anything but the briefest of adult–child interactions are even more limited. Yet if we are to support language development, we need to find ways of creating more of these opportunities; however busy we are, we need to carve out time to talk.

Television and DVDs are no substitute for interaction with real people. Research suggests that children under the age of two years are unlikely to benefit from children's TV in that, while they might find it visually stimulating, they will find it more difficult to acquire new vocabulary from that milieu than in face-to-face interactions (Close, 2004). Too much TV viewing also seems to affect children's attention and listening. Christakis *et al.* (2004) looked at the pre-school TV viewing habits of seven-year-olds in the USA, finding a 10 per cent increased risk of attention problems for every hour of television watched over and above the average pre-school level.

The way adults talk with children

The National Literacy Trust (2010) research report provides evidence that adults who take their lead from the child have a more positive effect on language development than those trying to direct the child. For example, more rapid vocabulary development in children is associated with adult input that picks up and follows the child's focus of attention rather than drawing the child's attention to something different. So commenting on what the child is doing is effective, as is responding to their utterances with what are called 'expansions' (adding to what they say) or 'recasts' (repeating back what they say in the right form but not correcting their speech). Table 2.1, adapted from one developed by the National Strategies, shows examples of the types of adult response that support language development in the early years.

Table 2.1 Adult responses which support language development

Child says/communicates	Adult responds	How does this response help?
Baby smiles when he sees dinner	Dinner! (several times)	Adult follows child's focus of attention. Gives child naming vocabulary and models next stage of language development.
Milk	Milk gone	This is an example of an expansion. The adult models a two-word sentence – the next stage in language development.
'Poon	Oh yes, a spoon… Daisy's spoon	This is an example of a recast. The adult models the correct form.
I've maked a tunnel	Yes, you've made a long, dark tunnel	Expansion and recast. The adult models the correct form and an extended vocabulary.
I need to make my track work	I wonder what shape you need it to be?	The adult tunes in to what the child is focusing on, and asks an open question, which models vocabulary and encourages the child to think and respond.

Reminiscing about events

One particularly effective form of developing young children's language is reminiscing about events that the child and their 'communication partner' have jointly experienced. This provides a motivating and meaningful context to move language on from describing the here and now to encompass things that are not actually present. It also helps children develop 'narrative' skills that research shows are very important throughout school.

I have become acutely aware of the power of reminiscence through my own recent experience of becoming a grandparent of twin boys. Early on, we put together in book format photographs of experiences we had shared with the boys. The first, 'Mending the wobbly post box', describes in pictures the day the boys helped their grandfather mend the box we have at the end of our drive for our mail to go in. The event involved real and toy toolboxes, a wheelbarrow, two dogs and all sorts of exciting measuring, hammering and screwing – real and pretend.

The next book is called 'When Isaac got locked in the toilet', and describes (again, without text) how on Christmas Day one of the twins managed to turn the key in the lock and get it firmly stuck when playing hide and seek, so that in the end Grandpa and Daddy had to kick the door down. Some photographs we took at the time, others at a later dramatic re-enactment.

These books are the first thing the boys ask for when we visit, so over and over again we go over the events – reinforcing the vocabulary, using the past tense, varying intonation with dramatic voices, exploring cause and effect and feelings, telling a bit of the story then handing over to one or other of the twins for the next. Their language development has come on in leaps and bounds as a result.

Sharing rhymes, songs and books

Another key factor that promotes language development is represented by activities such as sharing rhymes (such as nursery rhymes), playing rhyming games, singing familiar songs and sharing books.

Sharing books, particularly when it includes open-ended questions and encourages the child to respond, is a particularly powerful means of enhancing both children's spoken language skills and literacy development. We know from research that that the amount of time parents spent reading to their preschool children is strongly related to their language growth, as is the number of picture books in the home.

The effects are apparent for older children too. Simply reading books out loud daily – two or more times for the same book – and explaining some word meanings at each reading, means 'children can acquire eight to twelve word meanings per week at school – enough to maintain average vocabulary gains during the primary years if such programmes can be sustained over a school year' (Biemiller, 2007).

Independent reading also develops language skills; indeed, for older children it is the prime way in which they expand their vocabulary. Cunningham and Stanovitch (1991) found that even after accounting for general intelligence and decoding ability, reading volume (amount of time spent reading) contributed significantly and independently to vocabulary knowledge for students aged 10 to 12 years.

Avoiding background noise

Young children are not able to attend to more than one thing at a time, so their language development is held back in situations where they cannot focus on conversations and interaction because they are distracted by background noise.

Important research in the Bristol area (Roulstone et al., 2011) has found that the amount of time television (adult and child programmes) was on in the home when child was under two predicted achievement at school entry. As this time increased, so the child's score at school entry decreased.

Television is not the only source of background noise. Many early years settings have a policy of using nursery rhyme tapes to provide a friendly backdrop while children are playing, but this too limits children's ability to attend to what adults and other children are saying when they are joining the child's play.

Similarly, research examined in more detail in Chapter 4 shows that children and young people at all ages find it difficult to learn in environments where there is a high level of background noise.

Opportunities for interaction with other children

Given the busy lives we lead, with not enough time to talk and listen, it is fortunate that children do not acquire all their language from adults. Research shows that child-to-child speech plays an important role in the development of language. Even very young children (between one and two years old) will engage in sound play with others their age, and from two years on interacting with other children provides them with rich opportunities for language development: engaging in joint planning, negotiating conflicts, providing explanations, and telling each other stories.

Continued use of the home language when children are growing up bilingual

Research shows that children learning two languages develop language in the same way as children using one language. But they need a secure foundation in one language if they are to learn a second with ease.

A good summary of the evidence on bilingualism is provided in *Educating Second Language Children* (Genesee, 1994). Genesee reminds us that:

- bilingual acquisition is a common and normal childhood experience;
- all children are capable of learning two languages in childhood;
- knowing the language of one's parents is an important and essential component of children's cultural identity and sense of belonging;
- bilingual acquisition is facilitated if children have sustained, rich, and varied experiences in both languages;
- proficiency in both languages is more likely if children have sustained exposure in the home to the language that is used less extensively in the community (the language that is used more widely will get support outside the home); and
- parents can facilitate bilingual proficiency by using the language they know best and by using it in varied and extensive ways.

These findings have profound significance for educators. Learning to be a capable communicator in the language of the home means that children develop the language structures, the understandings about language and the vocabulary to which they can link the new learning in the second language. They develop transferable skills. It also means that children have access to the rich interactions with parents and other family members who may not be fluent in English which, as we have seen above, promote linguistic development.

The most disadvantaged children are those who, because of an insistence on an English-only approach, do not early on develop a proficiency in either English or their home language. For them, the path to lifelong language learning will have been seriously disrupted.

The features of communication-supportive classrooms

One offshoot of the 2008 Bercow Review of services for children with SLCN (the review which led to my role as Communication Champion) was substantial government funding for a programme of research on speech, language and communication needs – the 2009–12 Better Communication Research Programme. The programme was multi-stranded and one element (the Communication Supporting Classrooms Project, reported in Lindsay et al., 2011) sought to develop a tool which could capture the dimensions which promote oral language development in classrooms.

First, the researchers undertook a comprehensive review of the literature. From this they derived three dimensions (Figure 2.2): the language learning environment (the physical environment and learning context), language learning opportunities (the *what* of learning – the structured opportunities that are present in the setting to support language development) and language learning interactions (the *how* of learning – the ways in which adults in the setting talk with children). They then developed and trialled a classroom observation tool for Reception and Key Stage 1 based on these dimensions. Extracts from the tool are shown in Table 2.2. The full tool can be found at www.talkoftheschool.org.uk.

Of particular interest are the results from the trialling of the tool in classrooms – over a hundred classrooms across the country. As Figure 2.3 shows, the lowest-scoring area in all age groups was language learning opportunities. There were no significant differences between

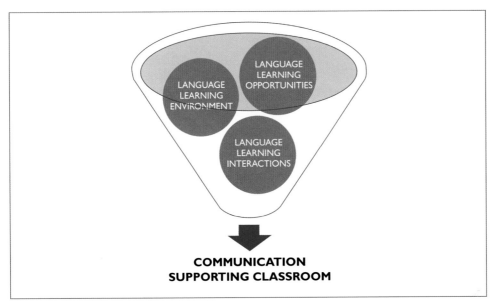

Figure 2.2 Dimensions of a communication supporting classroom

Source: Lindsay *et al.* (2011)

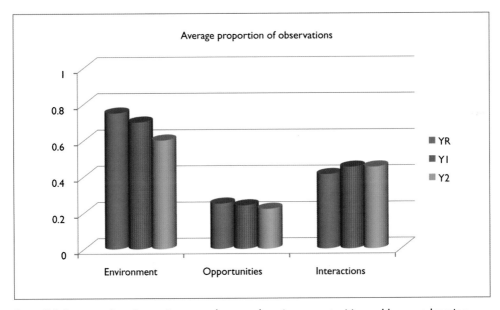

Figure 2.3 Language learning environment, language learning opportunities and language learning interactions

Reception, Y1 and Y2 for language learning opportunities and language learning interactions, but language learning environment showed a steep decline in quality over the year groups. Classes in urban schools scored lower on language learning opportunities than rural schools.

Table 2.2 Extract from Better Communication Research Programme classroom observation tool

Dimensions	Not seen	Observed	Reported at interview	N/A	Comments/ example
Language learning opportunities	*This dimension involves the structured opportunities that are present in the setting to support language development*				
Small group work takes place					
Interactive book reading takes place					
Children have opportunities to engage in structured conversations with teachers and other adults					
Children have opportunities to engage in structured conversations with peers (talking partners)					
Good quality toys, small world objects and real/ natural resources are available					
Musical instruments, noise makers and puppets are available					
Children have opportunities to engage in dressing- up/role play					

Small-group work facilitated by an adult was the most common form of language learning opportunity observed, and interactive book reading the least – even though much research shows that this is a powerful way of developing language.

The researchers also charted the types of adult interactions with children that they observed in classrooms. The most common behaviours observed were using children's names to get their attention, use of natural gesture, acknowledging and confirming children's contributions, and using open questions. The least common were specific praise for listening skills, encouraging turn-taking, and use of frames/scripts to scaffold children's talk (e.g. in role-play areas).

Practitioners might want to use these findings to reflect on their own practice. Are there language-learning opportunities that are missing, for example, and could be introduced? Are there forms of interaction that could be changed?

Communication-supporting classrooms in secondary schools

Research has not yet been done to map secondary schools' language-learning environments, opportunities and interactions through classroom observations like those undertaken for Reception and Key Stage 1 in the Better Communication Research Programme. So it is not yet possible to draw any conclusions about what secondary teachers typically do and don't do.

Nevertheless, a tool similar to the primary classroom observation tool has been developed at Sheffield University as part of the evaluation of a programme called Secondary Talk, which is delivered by the children's communication charity ICAN. The tool is grounded in the research literature and can be found in the 'Classroom approaches' section of the Leadership resources on www.talkoftheschool.org.uk.

The tool defines three key areas of a communication-supportive classroom: talking to and communication with pupils, vocabulary teaching and general classroom practice. An extract from the vocabulary teaching section is shown in Table 2.3.

Again, this tool can be used as the basis for reflection and development of any areas of practice that need to be strengthened in order to promote language and communication skills.

Summary

In this chapter we have mapped some of the factors that help promote children's language development. We have considered key features of communication-supportive classrooms, and research that shows where there may be gaps in current practice. In the chapters that follow, we will look at examples of good practice that demonstrate how some of the most common gaps identified in the research might be addressed. These are grouped into a place to talk (corresponding to language learning environments), a reason to talk and teaching talk (corresponding to language learning opportunities), and finally support for talk (corresponding to language learning interactions). First, we will hear about some case study schools whose practice exemplifies all of these key elements.

Table 2.3 Extract from secondary classroom observation measure

Section 3 : Teaching vocabulary			
Skill	**Description of skill**	**Rating**	**Comments**
1.	The teacher specifies what the new words to learn are	1 2 3 4 5	
2.	The teacher explicitly teaches the new vocabulary before the words are embedded into the lesson (e.g. provides a definition/ focuses on the semantic features or meaning(s) of the word)	1 2 3 4 5	
3.	The teacher focuses on the meaning of the new words and links the new words to other words/experiences the pupils are already familiar with	1 2 3 4 5	
4.	The teacher focuses on the phonological structure of the new words word (i.e. what the word sounds like and the sounds in the word)	1 2 3 4 5	
5.	The teacher uses visual support while teaching new vocabulary (e.g. pictures, photographs, symbols)	1 2 3 4 5	
6.	The teacher repeats the new vocabulary frequently	1 2 3 4 5	
7.	The teacher gives pupils opportunities to practice the new words (e.g. saying them before writing them)	1 2 3 4 5	
8.	The teacher encourages pupils to ask questions and to seek clarification about the new words	1 2 3 4 5	

Source: Classroom observation measure from Clegg *et al.* (2011)

Stories from schools

The inspirational examples of effective work on language and communication which I saw in schools and settings across the country in my time as Communication Champion all seemed to have one thing in common: a multi-level approach. By this I mean that the schools and settings invariably worked at three levels, or 'waves': everyday classroom curriculum practice, 'catch-up' interventions for groups of children, and more specialist interventions for those with the greatest difficulties. In many cases the schools and settings also built strong partnerships with parents/carers in their vital role supporting their children's language development.

Waves of intervention

This multi-level Wave 1/2/3 approach (see box below) will be familiar to most of us now, in relation to literacy, maths and social and emotional learning. The effective settings I saw, however, were unusual in also having a well-articulated map of what would happen for communication and language at each of the three waves.

To check your own Wave 1 provision, you might like to ask yourself the following questions:

- Do all staff know how, at Wave 1, they can make the physical environment communication-friendly?
- Have they had training on how to 'talk so kids will listen, and listen so kids will talk'?
- Do they build speaking and listening objectives into their everyday planning?

If not, this might be a good place to start in your school improvement planning. Good Wave 1 language environments and adult models will not only help the high numbers of children with SLCN. They will also raise standards for the growing numbers of children learning English as an additional language. They are the foundation of good practice; focusing on just the additional help children might need at Wave 2 and 3 is rather like what a colleague called 'the pudding without the main course'. Inclusive, high-quality everyday classroom teaching should always be children's main diet.

Wave 2 provision was, I found from my travels, often a significant gap. While most schools have some sort of additional, time-limited 'catch up' provision for children with reading or maths difficulties, for language there is often nothing between what happens in the everyday classroom (Wave 1) and 'he/she needs to see a speech and language therapist'. Yet in the best practice I saw – described in the case studies below – schools and settings were meeting the broad range of language needs through their own provision.

The 'Waves' model of intervention

The model starts from the premise that Wave 1 is the effective inclusion of all pupils in high-quality learning and teaching. This should be the starting point for any school reviewing their provision.

The model enables systematic planning of provision. The waves are ways of categorising provision, not pupils.

Wave 1

Wave 1 is high-quality inclusive teaching supported by effective whole-school policies and frameworks, clearly targeted to all pupils' needs and prior learning.

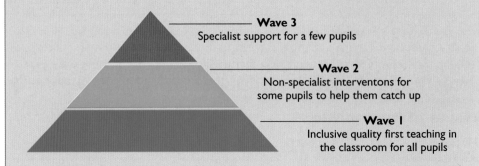

Wave 3
Specialist support for a few pupils

Wave 2
Non-specialist interventons for some pupils to help them catch up

Wave I
Inclusive quality first teaching in the classroom for all pupils

Figure 3.1 Waves of intervention

Wave 2

Wave 2 is Wave 1 plus additional and time-limited interventions provided for some children who need help to accelerate their progress, to enable them to work at or above age-related expectations. This usually takes the form of a structured programme of small-group support, carefully targeted and delivered by teachers or teaching assistants who have the skills to help pupils achieve their learning objectives. This can occur outside (but in addition to) whole-class lessons, or be built into mainstream lessons as part of guided work. Critically, intervention support needs to help pupils apply their learning in mainstream lessons. Intervention programmes need to be closely monitored to ensure that they meet pupils' needs.

Wave 3

Wave 3 is Wave 1 plus increasingly individualised programmes, based on independent evidence of what works. Wave 3 describes additional targeted provision for a minority of children where it is necessary to provide highly tailored intervention to accelerate progress or enable children to achieve their potential. This may include one-to-one or specialist interventions.

This put them in a good position to meet recent changes to the SEN system, in which schools are asked to provide good support for all children with additional needs, while formally identifying fewer as having SEN. Adopting the three-Wave approach does this for SLCN. The large group who are held back from achieving in school simply because of restricted vocabulary or listening and attention problems can have their needs met through carefully planned Wave 1 and 2 provision. This leaves a smaller group with long-term persistent SLCN for whom the partnership between school, parents and speech and language therapist will ensure good, if slower, progress.

CASE STUDY

Watercliffe Meadow primary school in Sheffield was the winner of the 'Shine a light' award for communication-supportive primary school of the year during the national year of communication.

The head teacher and staff have a shared vision about the importance of meeting children's speech, language and communication needs – with good reason. In January 2010, 29 out of 39 children in the school's nursery, due to start their reception year in September 2010, had language levels of 18 months to 2 years 6 months on Early Years Foundation Stage (EYFS) assessments.

The school's strategy to tackle language needs includes working with parents/carers, good systems for identifying SLCN and tracking children's progress, and three waves of provision. There is an absolute expectation that all parents/carers will come into school for workshops when their children start nursery. The first workshop is aptly titled 'It's good to talk'. It includes the experience of trying to talk with a spoon in your mouth, to get across important messages about the use of dummies.

At **Wave 1,** the school uses some of the extra time they have bought in from the Sheffield speech and language therapy service to provide Hanen and Makaton training to all EYFS staff. The therapist has also modelled a number of different language interventions with groups (such as 'Play and Say'). Staff have embedded these into their everyday practice with all children.

The curriculum is rich with visits and experiential learning to promote talk. The school uses approaches such as Pie Corbett's Talk for Writing, Philosophy for Children and Quality Circle Time to give children language structures that enable them to have deep conversations and discussions on issues that are important to them. The school café has 'social seating' to promote talk, and is open for parents at the start and end of the day, and throughout the day for children. The playground is also seen as a key opportunity; 'just as the teacher would structure conversation and debate in the classroom, we have a team of "play leaders" (mainly teaching assistants) who initiate games that encourage children to talk and interact', head teacher Ian Read explains.

At **Wave 2,** there are well-planned interventions to provide extra help for children who need it. In nursery and reception classes there are language groups that pre-teach key vocabulary a week before the children are going to meet it in a new topic. A speech and language therapy assistant runs speech groups, and the 'Talking Partners' small group intervention devised in Bradford runs in the Reception year to Year 4.

All children have their language skills assessed by the end of their first term in nursery. Their language progress is then individually tracked as they move up through the school. For example, the nursery assessment includes the British Picture Vocabulary Scale, which is repeated as children reach their fourth and fifth birthdays. Every half-term the speech and language therapist meets class teachers and goes through tracking data, identifying strategies to support children with SLCN in class, or further interventions. Children who are still having difficulties at the start of Y1 are prioritised for therapy at **Wave 3**.

The impact of the school's focus on communication has been noted by Ofsted: 'Achievement has improved substantially... This is most notable in developing speech and language in KS1, which is having a direct impact on attainment in reading and writing.'

CASE STUDY

During the national year of communication, the Communication Council – the national advisory group set up following the Bercow Review – marked the Hello campaign by visiting Over Hall primary school in Cheshire, to hear about the remarkable work of a cluster of schools (two special, ten primary and one academy) to tackle speech, language and communication issues across the town of Winsford. The schools purchase additional time from the local speech and language therapy service so that school-based therapists can help staff embed approaches such as narrative therapy and talking partners into their everyday teaching, assess children, and train and support designated teaching assistants to run intervention programmes. The schools also work with ICAN, who have arranged large-scale training events for staff across the cluster. In the early years, speech and language therapists and Children's Centres provide parents with a key ring of top tips for talk, with new tips added each week. There is also the 'lollipop challenge', when parents try talking with a lollipop in their mouths, to help them understand the impact of dummies.

Another cluster initiative is a research project, supported by Chester University, in which children formed a team to find out what makes a good conversation, observed conversations in classrooms, and now act as 'Conversation Champions' to coach and support their peers. The children involved were not initially the most confident or skilled communicators, yet when we visited they were able to make a superb presentation to the Council.

CASE STUDY

At Elizabeth Garrett Anderson Language College in Camden, staff have worked with the local speech and language therapy service to improve pupils' attainment by building their communication skills. Work is at three levels: individual therapy for pupils with significant difficulties, targeted small group work, and whole-school approaches to learning and teaching in classrooms. All Year 7 pupils have been screened, and those needing help with communication skills access six-week modules of small group work. There are modules on active listening and social communication skills. Speech and language therapists team-teach everyday lessons, working with one faculty at a time, and highlighting ways of adapting questioning styles, supporting pupil listening skills and developing the skills needed for group discussion. Science staff, for example, have focused on how to improve explanations through clearer definitions of terms and increased repetition. Each pupil and class involved is monitored carefully to evaluate the impact of the programme. Evidence to date shows improved learning and behaviour. Pupils describe the benefits as increased ability to listen and focus, and having an expectation now that they should understand what they hear in a lesson.

CASE STUDY

At Haverstock secondary school in Camden, the three waves are well embedded. The local speech and language therapy service works closely with the SENCO and learning support team. A specialist SEN teacher runs groups for pupils with SLCN. Professional development in the school is organised on a Teaching and Learning Communities (TLC) model, in which ten teachers work together for a year to make changes to their practice. The specialist SEN teacher leads a TLC that has adopted SLCN as a focus. Subject teachers have experimented with increased visual support for lessons, and adapted their own language. A consistent set of symbols has been introduced to illustrate elements of a lesson (class discussion, listening, group work, paired talk, using computers and so on). These appear on the whiteboard or sheets on students' desks at the start of a lesson, so that they know what to expect.

Speaking and listening skills are actively taught to all students, using games like '20 questions' and 'I went to Camden market and bought'. Posters remind students of core skills like looking at the speaker, taking turns, and asking for clarification if you don't understand. Withdrawal groups for students with SLCN provide more intensive work on these same skills.

CASE STUDY

Preston Manor, the winner of the Shine a Light award for communication-supportive secondary school of the year during the national year of communication, described how the English department worked with staff from the school's speech and language resource base to:

- develop speaking and listening lessons for all Year 7 and Year 8 students;
- provide training on adolescent speech, language and communication development to all newly qualified teachers;
- implement a national year of communication campaign with a logo designed by students, and a noticeboard displaying a communication focus of the week;
- devise a special lesson for *all* students, delivered in the spring term, in which they explored what it means to have a voice;
- devise new citizenship lessons for Y7 – on the unwritten rules of communication, constructive criticism, and negotiation and compromise;
- run targeted groups for expressive language, introductory social skills, vocabulary

enrichment and social skills/life skills, with information for all staff on the groups available; and

- make a film about speech and language to be used in further staff training next year.

In addition, small group interventions were developed for expressive language strategies, vocabulary enrichment and social skills. The school has a Targeted Groups working party and a booklet for staff that communicates what groups are available for students. All group materials (PowerPoint slides, agendas, games) are accessible to all school staff via the intranet.

The school has also recently worked with the charity ICAN on its Secondary Talk programme. One initiative has been to introduce whole-class Talk Targets in English lessons, such as 'Challenging other people's opinions gently without starting an argument', or 'Knowing when not to add anything else to the conversation.' At the end of the lesson, pupils discuss whether they have met the target, and where they still need to improve.

Making change happen in the early years

All the case study schools described above realised that developing a multi-level approach to language and communication would involve changing some fairly entrenched adult behaviours. As adults and professionals, we have developed and practised particular ways of communicating with children and young people over many years. These styles of communication become, in a sense, part of 'how we are', as automatic as driving a car becomes after an equivalent period.

Changing established behaviour is difficult, for a teacher or any professional. It requires effort and time, and a good deal more than just 'going on a course'. What I saw working well, therefore, was sustained professional development, in which training was followed up with the chance to try out new ideas in the setting, with support, and reflect on the impact.

I was particularly impressed here by the Every Child a Talker programme, which has much to teach us about how to change adult behaviours. Each pre-school setting involved had a 'lead practitioner' whose role was to champion change across the setting. The lead practitioner attended external training delivered by experts such as speech and language therapists. They then worked alongside colleagues in their setting (or beyond) in a coaching role, and took part in regular network meetings where they could share practice with other lead practitioners. Staff filmed themselves with children, talked to colleagues about the video, made small changes to their practice, then filmed themselves again. As one practitioner put it: 'The video was a real revelation. It was clear I simply talked too much and didn't give children enough time to respond. I also asked far too many questions!'

Practitioners in many cases transformed the way they interacted with children. Instead of interrogating them, they learned to make comments that open up conversation. So instead of asking 'Did you like the story?', for example, they would say things like 'Do you know, I really liked the bit in the story when the girl found her dog...', and wait for a response. They learned, too, how to build language by repeating back what children say in expanded form, so that if a child says 'Teddy bed' they might respond with 'Yes, Teddy's sleeping in the bed'. They learned how to use 'recasting' – expanding the child's language in correct and more mature form so that if a child says, for example, 'He hitted the ball and it went really far and...and...', the adult might reply 'Yes, he hit the ball really hard and it went really far, so he had to go and look for it'.

Another useful tool in Every Child a Talker was peer coaching – partnering up with another practitioner and asking them to observe their colleague's interactions with children and provide feedback. Table 3.1 provides an observation tool to help with this, which I saw used in Warrington. Here, the tool was used by a practitioner and their peer coach when watching a video of the practitioner interacting with a child. The practitioner set the agenda for the observation, and might say, for example, 'I want to know if I ask too many questions'. After watching the video the coach would give their partner one piece of positive feedback, then show them what they had noted on the observation form – a count of how many questions were asked versus comments made, examples of getting down to the child's level to communicate, examples of giving the child time to respond, and so on.

A similar model was used in Islington. The lead practitioners attended training on the theory behind language development and adult–child interaction, watching film clips of themselves and using a tally sheet and list of prompts and questions to reflect with a partner on their interactions with children. Each practitioner then identified an interaction strategy they wanted to use more, and put this into practice with support from their partner. Later, they set up the coaching model with other staff in their own settings. Results showed a significant decrease in the numbers of pupils with delayed language.

Making change happen in the primary phase

Many schools and local authorities are now taking the learning from Every Child a Talker into Key Stage 1 and 2, with Communication Champions in primary schools, and the use of peer observation and coaching. Table 3.2 provides an observation tool that might be useful here.

A successful model of making change happen was used by Foley Park Primary in Worcestershire (a runner up in the Shine a Light 'Hello' communication-friendly school of the year award). Here, just one new strategy was introduced to staff each half term. Staff would have a short input from a speech and language therapist on – say – the 'ten second rule' (wait ten seconds after asking a question before expecting an answer). They would then be supported by a school-based member of staff leading on the project, who might observe them in class and provide feedback. Another half-term was spent on special ways of identifying key topic vocabulary ('Goldilocks' words – not too easy, not too hard, but just right; see Table 6.1 in Chapter 6), teaching these words using a multisensory approach and then applying and reviewing them. Another half-term focused on visual support; staff could drop in on the school's well-equipped Chatterbox room for practical help with adding pictures, photos and symbols to classroom resources.

Action research is another useful tool I saw used to promote changes in behaviour. At Over Hall primary school in Cheshire, children were involved in researching what happened in classrooms and presenting their findings. They found that children often didn't understand what the teacher was saying. They also reported that 'We – the children – are very good at talking but not so good at listening.' From this came a staff development programme on how to modify adult language ('chunking' instructions, using visual supports and so on), and work in classes on listening skills. At the end, children repeated their classroom observations and found positive changes.

Table 3.1 Every Child a Talker: reflecting on practice in Warrington

Play	Never	Some-times	Often	All the time
Does the practitioner:				
Sit where they can easily make eye contact?				
Let the children choose the toy/activity?				
Join in with the children's play?				

Communicating	Never	Some-times	Often	All the time
Does the practitioner:				
Use appropriate eye contact and facial expression?				
Adapt spoken language level according to situation?				
Give children enough time to talk/wait for them to start the interaction?				
Make comments on the child's actions?				
Model correct speech/language?				
Expand/build on the child's sentences and ideas?				
Make positive comments/give specific praise?				
Use more comments than questions/ instructions?				
Ensure an equal child–adult balance of conversational 'turns'?				

Table 3.2 Reflecting on practice: a peer coaching model for school staff

Question	Answer	Comment
Did I talk more than the pupils – how much of the time was spent in teacher talk? Pupil talk?		
How many questions did I ask?		
How many open/closed questions?		
How many complex sentences (with connectives) did I use?		
How long did I typically wait before expecting a reply to questions?		
Did I pause between instructions or chunks of speech?		
Did I expand/build on pupils' sentences and ideas?		
Did I ask them to tell me if they hadn't understood?		
Did I actively teach important new vocabulary – not just by explaining it once?		

A group of schools in Croydon used another powerful strategy – lesson study – to achieve sustained change in classrooms.

CASE STUDY

Talk for Learning was an initiative involving Croydon schools, local authority consult-ants and outside experts from the Thinkwell organisation. Each school nominated a lead or leads who took part in training sessions, beginning with a two-day launch event and training on how children develop speaking and listening skills, using talk to promote thinking, and on the lesson study model.

Participants then had a day in school to plan a staff meeting about the initiative and to plan their first lesson study on a chosen focus – for example, helping children develop questioning skills.

In lesson study, a pair or group of staff (such as phase leader and class teacher) plan a lesson together. Staff observe the children and each other over the course of the lesson, provide feedback and reflect together on the learning. Crucially, lesson study asks child-ren for their views on the lesson and how successful the teaching was.

Teachers taking part in the initiative also had the opportunity to pay a visit to observe a leading teacher or Advanced Skills Teacher at work. They met regularly to share the learning from their lesson studies, and take part in further training – for example in using drama, and the 'Talk for Writing' approach.

The schools involved used before and after observations to evaluate the impact of their work. The results showed that this way of working was really changing the way teachers interacted with their classes.

At Coulsdon Church of England primary school, for example, staff focused on developing children's skills in paired and group discussion, reflecting on what others have said, and questioning skills. One lesson study used the school's enterprise focus as a starting point. Children analysed what makes a pitch for funding for a new product effective, using film from *Junior Dragons' Den*, then worked in mixed ability groups of three to devise their own pitch to a bank manager.

Another lesson study asked children to place themselves on an 'opinion line' to show their response to a news report that PE might be taken out of the school curriculum. They then listened and responded to others' points of view and used the opinion line again at the end of the lesson to show whether their opinions had changed.

Staff drew on the training they had experienced to try out new strategies in the lessons – like the 'Because Bar', which encourages children to explain the reasons for their point of view, and 'Number 1–5', which allocates each child in a group discussion a number, so that the teacher can choose a number and that child will feed back on their group's discussion to the whole class.

Change was measured by auditing the percentage of teacher talk and pupil talk over a series of lesson studies. Findings showed that teacher talk decreased from 35 to 25 per cent, and pupil talk rose from 65 to 75 per cent. Pupils reported changes ('Talk for Learning has made me less chatty, made me think about my talk in the classroom', said one Year 3 pupil), as did parents ('I've noticed that Scott has started to say things like 'I can see what you're saying but...' and 'I can see what you mean, but what about...' and 'What do you mean by...?').

Making change happen in the secondary phase

At the other end of the age range, ICAN, the children's communication charity, have developed an interesting model of change for secondary schools. Secondary Talk is a whole-school approach linked to self-evaluation. It enables departments or individuals to choose a focus, then undertake a short self-study module (like 'Tweaking teacher talk', or 'Making homework more effective'), before making and reviewing small changes to their classroom practice. Secondary Talk is a coaching and mentoring model, rather than training, and that is what makes it effective. It is also flexible, recognising that those within the school are the experts about that school and about where the windows of opportunity for change might be.

External evaluation by the University of Sheffield has shown significant impact. The majority of school staff taking part were independently observed to make positive changes to their classroom practice by using more appropriate teacher talk, and actively helping pupils learn new vocabulary. Following Secondary Talk, pupils felt that teachers were easier to understand and used more visual support strategies which helped their learning. Staff reported improvements in learning and behaviour.

CASE STUDY

Kat Wilkes, Assistant Director of English/Literacy Coordinator at South Wolverhampton and Bilston Academy, describes how her school engaged with Secondary Talk. Step 1 involved staff in collectively identifying what they saw as the key language needs for their students, and choosing a relevant Secondary Talk 'Standard' to work towards. Drawing on the Secondary Talk resource manual, with advice from an ICAN consultant and bearing in mind what was workable in school where there was always the risk of initiative overload, Kat then chose a small number of approaches for staff to try out and evaluate on an action research basis. These included developing students' vocabulary, and helping them learn to work effectively in groups.

Departments went away and made laminated 'placemats' for students' desks, with key vocabulary, and subject-specific and generic frames to support talk and writing (how to argue a point, how to give an explanation, how to write a letter). Students worked to 'talk targets' when working in groups – taking turns to speak, making sure everyone gave their opinion, asking each other questions, using the key words related to the topic – and pupils identified as observers would use a Secondary Talk tick box and comments chart (Table 3.3) to record whether each group member was meeting the target.

Table 3.3 Secondary Talk tick box and comments chart

Talk Targets	Pupil 1	Pupil 2	Pupil 3	Pupil 4	Observer comments
Take turns to speak?					
Make sure everyone said their opinion?					
Ask each other questions?					
Use the key words relating to the topic?					

Schemes of work were modified to include opportunities for discussions using talk targets, scaffolding talk with talk frames, and use of placemats with key vocabulary.

Another interesting piece of action research focused on improving the way students were asked to reflect after incidents of poor behaviour or conflict. Previously, students used a sheet of paper with a couple of headings in which they wrote their account of events. This worked well for verbally fluent pupils, but penalised those who found it hard to articulate their thoughts. Staff wanted to scaffold the process for these students by giving them a visual frame (an 'Incident Narrative' from www.makesensetraining.co.uk; see also Chapter 7 for another possible model) to help them describe what happened, what the feelings were, what happened and what might have happened if they had made other choices.

CASE STUDY

The Spinney Centre is a secondary provision in Coventry, for boys with behavioural, emotional and social difficulties. Auditing the boys' needs, staff found that two-thirds had some sort of communication difficulty. Secondary Talk enabled them to evaluate current practice and make changes. Lesson observations by external consultants showed that teacher talk predominated in class. Staff then 'asked ourselves why we felt the need to fill the silences' and realised that the answer lay in their own fear of things getting out of control if they did not fill every minute. Talk was being used as a way of managing behaviour. Staff also observed that they tended to ask students closed questions they could easily answer in very few words, so as to avoid putting them in a position of anxiety – again, with the probability that this would lead to behaviour problems.

Observations showed that students looked to staff to negotiate their group and pairs tasks; they weren't able to work independently in any sort of group. 'Many of the boys have low self-esteem and fragile confidence and rely on others to speak for them. Overall they had very little verbal independence in lessons and this needed to change', said head teacher Annie Tindale.

Bit by bit, staff introduced changes like teaching students to work in small groups, and using the 'ten second rule' – waiting ten full seconds after asking a student a question, in order to give them time to process the information. Staff were anxious about this, but students found it very helpful. One exceptionally quiet teenager paused for a whole minute before answering a question, but got it correct.

The majority of school staff who took part in Secondary Talk were independently observed to make positive changes to their classroom practice as a result of their action research. They talked less, gave students more thinking time, got better at facilitating more supportive general classroom discussion, made more use of visual support and introduced more structured group work.

Accreditation

Schools and settings have, I found, made change happen most effectively when they are enabled to work towards a goal. Useful here is the Communication Trust's framework of competencies in supporting language and communication (available at www.communicationhelppoint.org.uk), which can be completed online, and allows anyone working with children and young people to evaluate their skills and knowledge about communication. They can then identify areas where they want to develop. In addition, whole settings can access the online assessment with a designated group number and collectively assess their developmental training needs. The competencies are divided into stages: universal (the basic skills and knowledge that everyone working with children and young people should have) through to enhanced, then specialist, then extension (the specialised learning around speech, language and communication needs required by someone working or studying at a post-graduate level).

Working towards an actual external award or accreditation can be very powerful in driving change. ICAN's Early Talk, Primary Talk and Secondary Talk are examples of such accreditation, with standards to work towards at three levels – universal, enhanced and specialist.

The Elklan organisation also provide accreditation to schools if they engage in a package consisting of:

- a ten-week Open College Network accredited speech and language support in the class-room course for at least two teaching assistants;
- a course for SENCO and a class teacher, for three days run over three terms;
- a Communication Counts course (three one-hour sessions) cascaded by the SENCO to all staff; and
- a communication-friendly school audit.

Similarly, several local authorities, such as Stoke-on-Trent, Sheffield and North Lincolnshire, have devised their own awards for communication supportive environments. Sheffield's awards are linked to the completion, over time, of an Every Sheffield Child articulate and literate communication-friendly school audit structured around the three waves and enabling schools to audit their practice under the dimensions of leadership and management, Wave 1 provision (social ethos), Wave 1 provision (teaching and learning), Wave 1 provision (learning environment), Wave 2 and Wave 3 provision, and the involvement of parents and carers. This useful audit tool can be found at the Communication Trust's 'Talk of the school' website (www.talkoftheschool.org.uk), under the leadership resources tab.

Summary

In this chapter we have looked at examples of settings and schools that have transformed their practice and embedded a multi-level approach, which means every child gets the support they need as they learn to communicate. We have also looked at what helped them on this journey.

Summing up, the key features of making that difficult leap towards different ways of communicating in settings and classrooms are as follows:

- An in-school or setting lead practitioner – like the Every Child a Talker lead practitioner, a Communication Champion, or ambassadors for talk in each subject department.
- An 'enthusiastic vanguard' – a small group of staff who will try out new things and spread enthusiasm to others.
- Access to external expertise – training and support from an advisory teacher and/or speech and language therapist.
- Some process involving auditing current practice through classroom observation or video.
- Some process involving reflective practice (coaching, action research, lesson study).
- A way of evaluating impact, particularly seeking children and young people's views, as this can be highly motivating if their feedback is good.
- A goal to work towards, such as accreditation.

We now move on to what good practice looks like in Wave 1 approaches – everyday practice in classrooms and settings that provide a real 'place to talk' (and listen) through their learning environment.

4 A place to talk

Introduction

In this chapter we look at what we know about how language develops, and how this can be applied to the learning environment so that it provides the optimum conditions for talking and listening.

First, let me tell you about Derwentwater primary school in Ealing, which exemplified for me what we mean by 'a place to talk' more than any other setting I visited.

CASE STUDY

Derwentwater has high numbers of EAL learners and above average levels of social deprivation. Language was a priority, so it seemed right to take part in the Every Child a Talker initiative.

One of the first steps the school took was to look at the environment in the Foundation Stage, to see how children were using the spaces. They found that the more open the space, the noisier it became, and the more it was dominated by confident children. The more intimate the space, the more those children who were relatively lacking in confidence felt able to engage, and the more children talked to adults and each other – and could be heard. So staff planned ways of breaking up the space, creating a corner of the playground with trellis and drapes, and putting in small play houses. Noticing that children are stimulated to talk by strong sensory experiences, they created a sensory garden full of things to look at, smell, touch and listen to. They also built a little bridge between the main playground area and the garden, where children are often to be seen 'guarding' the bridge – and having conversations with other children as they cross over.

Audits also showed that role play, problem solving and investigation were the activities that were most likely to lead to collaboration and communication. So role-play areas were carefully planned, like a wonderful baby clinic with several telephones for children to use to make appointments, and visual support – a bank of pictures on the wall (such as a syringe and bandages) that children could point to say how they wanted their 'baby' treated if they did not know the word. Role play was linked to problem-solving and investigation, and to indoor and outdoor play; a group of boys, for example, decided that the babies in the baby clinic needed washing, so they discussed how they could do this, finding a large, empty planting bucket and working out how to fill it with water.

Adults undertook training and learned how to change some habitual ways of interacting with children. All staff learned Makaton. Instead of asking questions, they learned to comment on what children were doing, to give children time to respond, to be aware of the length of their own utterances and whether this was appropriate to a child's language level. Comments practitioners could use to encourage talk ('That's really interesting... I wonder how... You've used...') were displayed on the wall in areas where staff had in the past found it hardest to use appropriate open-ended language. Staff discussed and agreed on the key vocabulary they wanted children to learn for particular activities; these words were written on cards and hung above that activity (for example, 'falling', 'scatter', 'filling', 'pouring' above a table of seeds, beans, funnels and bottles).

Language-rich environments

Language-rich environments, like those at Derwentwater, provide spaces that actively encourage talking and listening – chat-inducing spaces.

Every setting, school and classroom has 'communication hotspots', where much talk and listening goes on, and 'coldspots', where there is little. In the Every Child a Talker programme, practitioners were encouraged to observe children at play to identify these spaces in their own setting. They made a map of the setting layout (inside and outside), marking each area – construction, climbing frame, sand, mark-making and so on. They then observed children and put coloured crosses on their map to mark the hotspots for talking: one cross for places where talking takes place sometimes, more crosses if more often. With another coloured pen they marked places where they thought more talking could take place.

Once coldspots had been identified, practitioner made plans for change. One setting, for example, noticed that in the outside area the children were spending most of their time riding round and round on bikes and cars, but not talking, so they turned a coldspot into a hotspot by setting up a pit-stop area with tools one day, and an improvised petrol pump made with bendy washing machine tubes attached to the fence on another. Other settings have developed den-making boxes for children to carry to a chosen space to make a den. One early years setting in Stoke-on-Trent turned a fence between the setting and the primary school playground into a talking hotspot by the simple device of attaching ribbons to the fence for children on each side to thread.

Simple changes can make all the difference, like not having all the equipment out for an activity, so children have to ask for what they want. Just defining an outdoor space with a circle of tree stumps, putting out a circular table with four chairs round it, or putting old mobile phones are all immediate conversation creators. Practitioners have revamped book areas to include story props and puppets, and introduced MP3 players like Story Phones and Easi-Ears, placing headsets loaded with space stories and sounds in a dark den during a space project, for example. At Magdalen Gates pre-school in Norwich, staff developed 'Step into a Story' communication-friendly spaces where children could imagine stepping into a page of a favourite book – like an 'owl babies' area with tree branches, toy owls, books, cushions and baskets of conkers and leaves.

Other settings have looked at their displays and made them more interactive, such as by introducing 'Discovery bottles' – large plastic bottles filled with materials that encourage children to explore and discuss (like a wave bottle, half filled with cooking oil and a quarter filled with water plus blue food colouring – as you turn the bottle on its side, the waves roll gently).

A primary school turned grounds and corridors into hotspots by involving the children in coming up with a collection of open-ended questions like 'What do you do when you are bored?', or 'What animal would you like to be?'. These were then put up on walls and paths in the school grounds and corridors, and regularly changed as children came up with new ideas.

Other ways of auditing the environment

As well as auditing the environment, Every Child a Talker encouraged practitioners to audit the extent to which daily routines and activities promote talk. Practitioners drew a time line listing everything that happened during the setting's day. For example:

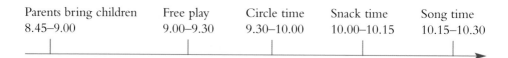

Parents bring children	Free play	Circle time	Snack time	Song time
8.45–9.00	9.00–9.30	9.30–10.00	10.00–10.15	10.15–10.30

They then again marked the talking hotspot times in one colour, and the times where more talking could take place with another.

Finally, practitioners looked at groups of children and at individuals to see where and when they were using talk. In Wolverhampton, for example, one children's centre tracked boys' activities and found that they centred in a few areas, with a main pathway between the construction area and the garden. Boys rarely approached adults, and adults, it seemed, rarely joined their play. Observations showed that there was on average less than one adult–child interaction per boy per session. This helped staff to understand why data also showed significant language delay among these boys, and they were able to make changes in interactions as a result.

I would love to see these audits of time and environment carried out by primary and secondary schools. The results could be illuminating. Watercliffe Meadow primary school, which we met in Chapter 3, for example, made the time when parents drop off their children into a hotspot through the café they introduced into their reception area. Schools in North Yorkshire did the same for lunch times, by putting conversation starters on tables at lunchtime and having staff on tables to facilitate talk.

Outdoor areas

Outdoor areas provide brilliant opportunities for talk. There are primary schools that have created a platform outside which children can use to re-enact stories or create their own plays, and schools (like Hookstone Chase in North Yorkshire) that have developed a 'chatterbox stop' in the playground, supervised by trained lunchtime supervisors, where children can take part in specific activities designed to promote social interaction. Forest schools, of course, give children very special opportunities to explore in a natural environment – building campfires, making dens, bird houses, hedgehog homes, mud castles and sculptures – and are brilliant for promoting language.

CASE STUDY

At Townsend Children's Centre in Bournemouth the outdoor area was jointly planned and created with parents, who found stones for a gravel pit and chose flowers for the garden. Dads built a 'bug hotel'; there are big tree stumps, a mud kitchen, a tunnel, 'fairy holes', chunky chains with padlocks and keys, and spaces within the gardens which provide quiet havens. Activities are planned for the outside area, such as growing vegetables and making lunch. Staff note the effects on children's communication skills: 'We tried den making with the dad's group and have seen how this has helped children's progress in language and speech. Children have quickly started to develop two-word phrases, closely followed by stringing sentences together' (Ofsted, 2011a).

Beyond the school or setting

Language-rich environments do not just apply to nurseries and schools. Any setting can take a look at how communication-supportive the environment is. Stoke-on-Trent's museum service provides a good example. As part of the 'Stoke Speaks Out' initiative, the museum service undertook staff training, then audited the museum environments. As a result, they introduced family trails, treasure baskets of objects for children to explore and talk about, boxes of costumes and even a tree that you can go inside. There is a very interesting *Communication Friendly Museums* booklet about this work and its impact on the museums' website at www.stokemuseums.org.uk.

Another wonderful project I saw was an initiative by the Imperial War Museum in Manchester, where staff had training and support from Elizabeth Jarman, then undertook an audit of their space. They re-organised their café so that families could sit together, put comfortable, low-level seating around the museum to encourage lingering and talk, introduced story-telling in their learning studio and brought in den-making equipment to create spaces where families could take books and artefacts.

Enclosed spaces

If I asked you where you would choose to go to meet a friend for a good chat, it is likely you would choose somewhere fairly private (but not too intimate) and comfortable. Starbucks is a frequent choice.

This illustrates adults' views on the 'chat-inducing' properties of spaces that feel small in scale and semi-enclosed. The same goes for children. They too will gravitate to a den, a corner with drapes, an enormous cardboard box and so on, to talk to each other or conduct their own running commentary on play with small toys. The photographs at the end of this chapter show some of these spaces. You will see that as well as being enclosed, the spaces are often furnished with soft and comfortable materials. Introducing softness noticeably increases what Elizabeth Jarman calls 'linger time'.

Early-years practitioners have responded to this message with enthusiasm, re-arranging the spaces in their setting so as to create more areas like these, out of the way of through traffic.

I saw comfy places created out of an old sofa with a throw and cushions, bean bags, and even a couple of large dog baskets with cushions, placed at an angle to each other so two children could nestle and talk.

To create the structure for dens, children and practitioners have used everything from garden canes to old clothes horses, pop-up tents, a table on its side, and enormous cardboard boxes. String, pegs, clamps, tape and clothes pegs fix things together, and drapes might be camouflage netting, tarpaulins, tablecloths, blankets, shower curtains and all sorts of fabrics from spotty voile to velvet. Softened with cushions, fleeces, blankets and duvets, all that are then needed are props, like a flask and thermos and mugs, torches (including head torches) or fairy lights for atmosphere.

Elizabeth's Jarman's excellent *Place to Talk* booklets and YouTube videos provide inspiring photographic examples of spaces like these, which support communication. *A Place to Talk for Boys*, for example, has a garden where pathways were cut through grass left deliberately long, which led to smaller spaces where children could gather, and a makeshift tepee in a child-minder's lounge, with leaves and branches to which a child who loved small world play with toy dinosaurs could retreat. Elizabeth's company also sell time-saving resources to help create communication-friendly spaces – like the lovely 'Outside Bag' which has a range of items such as cushions, lidded boxes, a hanging light, clamps and Velcro ties, that can be put together quickly in a range of ways to transform 'coldspots' into engaging places for talk.

Role-play areas

The role-play area is another focus for talk, of course, and I have been overwhelmed by prac-titioners' creativity in devising everything from ice cream parlours to shoe shops to space stations.

Role play is not just for the early years. I was inspired to hear about work on oracy at Parliament Hill secondary school in London, where role play is used even at A level, and a primary school with a 'football manager's office' role-play area where a Year 6 class applied their maths learning to planning fixtures, working out transfer fees and making calls to bid for new players. At St Paul's Church of England primary in Manchester, Key Stage 2 classes share a role-play area outside the classrooms. They set up a travel agent area when working on a weather round the world topic, which was used in reading time by small groups from each class. At Redhill primary in Birmingham, the Year 4 teacher asked the caretaker to build her a simple wooden structure, which has become a museum during a topic on the Vikings, a World War II bomb shelter, then the booking office of the Titanic with a telephone for children to take calls from passengers' relatives. Best of all was a hide, when children were studying habitats. The structure was covered with astroturf and had slits for birdwatching; props included sleeping bags, spotters' guides and a tape of different birdsongs. Children can ask to use the role-play area if they have finished a piece of written work; it is also used during 'golden time' as a reward for those with the best attendance, and in the mornings before lessons start.

A number of Sheffield schools have developed role play throughout the school and given a description in their applications for the local ESCAL accreditation as a communication-friendly school (Figure 4.1).

Ofsted comment favourably on role play in Key Stage 2. For example, in a thematic report on excellent English teaching (Ofsted, 2011b) they note that at St Thomas of Canterbury primary school in Salford, staff had extended the positive impact of EYFS role-play work into other areas of the school:

> All classes have created role-play areas. At the time of the inspection, the Year 3 class had recreated Roald Dahl's writing hut while the Year 6 classroom featured an Anderson

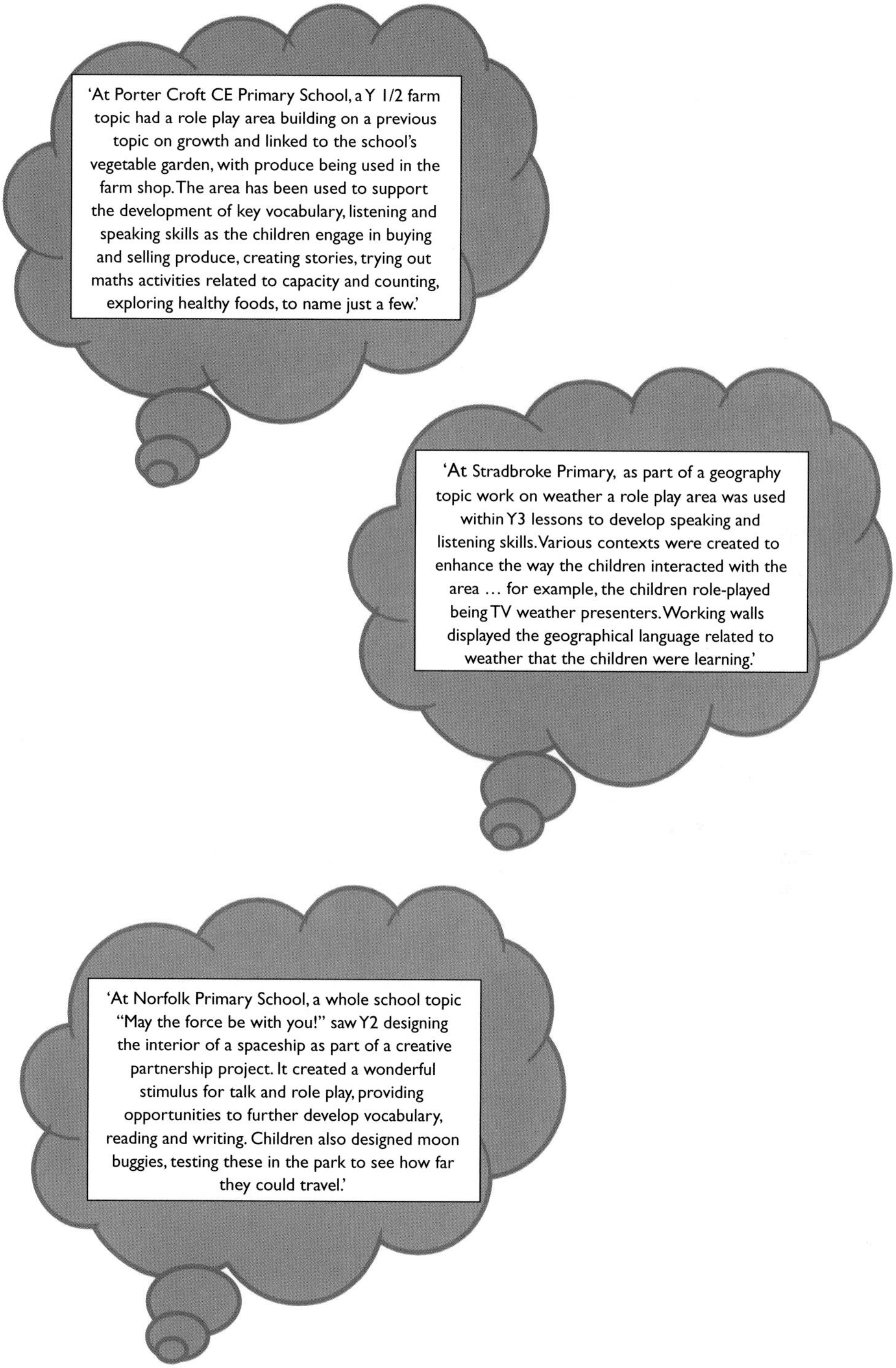

'At Porter Croft CE Primary School, a Y 1/2 farm topic had a role play area building on a previous topic on growth and linked to the school's vegetable garden, with produce being used in the farm shop. The area has been used to support the development of key vocabulary, listening and speaking skills as the children engage in buying and selling produce, creating stories, trying out maths activities related to capacity and counting, exploring healthy foods, to name just a few.'

'At Stradbroke Primary, as part of a geography topic work on weather a role play area was used within Y3 lessons to develop speaking and listening skills. Various contexts were created to enhance the way the children interacted with the area … for example, the children role-played being TV weather presenters. Working walls displayed the geographical language related to weather that the children were learning.'

'At Norfolk Primary School, a whole school topic "May the force be with you!" saw Y2 designing the interior of a spaceship as part of a creative partnership project. It created a wonderful stimulus for talk and role play, providing opportunities to further develop vocabulary, reading and writing. Children also designed moon buggies, testing these in the park to see how far they could travel.'

Figure 4.1 Role play in Sheffield primary schools

shelter as part of the history topic. These are used in different ways. For example, during one visit the Year 3 teacher and a group of pupils were pirates in their boat corner discussing how to scrub the decks and bury treasure. The role play here was intended to support the pupils' later instructional writing. In Year 5, a group of pupils dressed as doctors visited the 'laboratory' area to examine a skeleton in order to determine the cause of death; work that linked to their science topic. The Year 6 class had extended the work with their Second World War shelters into a drama about evacuation that was filmed and then used as a later teaching resource to support journalistic writing.

Using the role-play area to best effect

The best role-play areas are planned and designed by the children themselves. This is possible even at a young age. I saw a Reception class, for example, using a simple plan and cut-out shapes to design a layout for the role play area, and listing the props they would need the teachers to acquire. At Central primary school in Watford, Hertfordshire, children research the props they will need, for everything from an Egyptian pyramid to a post office and Tudor kitchen – for this they decided they needed menus, so sought out Tudor menus from the internet.

Simply providing a role play area is not enough to develop children's language. This requires an active role for the adult, to model for children ways in which they can use the area and appropriate vocabulary and language structures. At Central primary, a teacher or teaching assistant is always in the role play area when it is first set up, to model its use. The children then use the areas in guided reading times and during topic lessons.

At St Thomas of Canterbury primary, Ofsted noted the following:

> What is particularly effective is the school's use of role play to encourage good quality talk. Unlike many schools visited, this is identified as a priority and planned accordingly. Children are not left to 'get on with it themselves'. The teacher joins the role-play area and uses talk constantly to question, explain, motivate and model.

I saw many examples of role play areas used by practitioners in a conscious, planned way to develop children's language. In one setting I visited, for example, practitioners met every Friday to plan the vocabulary and language structures they wanted to model through adult interactions with children in the role play area. Planning like this gives developing children's language the same prominence as we give to planning for their literacy or mathematical development.

Small-world play and re-enacting stories

Small-world play with good resources linked to a recent language model (such as a story or theme) is another way of providing opportunities for children to use new vocabulary. A nice example I saw in Rotherham was a bag with a book about penguins, some small-world arctic animals, pretend ice bricks and sheets of material so that children could construct their own scene.

To develop language, it is important to have resources which prompt collaboration. Small worlds encourage this dialogue, and opportunities for children to learn from each other's talk. I came across this example in a lovely booklet of ideas called *A Sea of Talk*, produced by a group of schools in Sheffield.

Children were playing on a car mat with various vehicles, including police cars and break-down vehicles:

A: Oh no, the bikes have crashed, I'm gonna phone the police.

B: Phone for an ambulance too, looks as if the biker men are hurt.

C: Nee-naw, nee-naw, nee-naw. The police are here! What happened? Are there any witnesses to this accident?

A: No one saw it. I just heard the bang. Is the ambulance coming?

B: It's here now. No, don't take off the helmets. I heard on the telly their brains can fall out if it's dinted their heads.

C: Fall out where?

B: Anywhere, on't road, on't path.

C: Hey, ambulance is here. How many casualties? Any fatalities?

B: What are they?

C: What?

B: What you said.

C: Fatalities?

B: Yeah.

C: Dead people.

A: No, none of them. Just injuries.

On a larger scale, resources can be provided in the outdoor area for re-enacting a familiar story. For Michael Rosen's *We're Going on a Bear Hunt*, for example, practitioners put sleeping bags outside (to represent home), blue cloth (for the river), skipping ropes (swishy grass), a rain maker, branches for the forest, paper to tear up for a snowstorm, a big box to be a cave – and a camera.

Managing noise in the environment

As we saw in Chapter 2, background noise disrupts young children's language learning. This applies to older children, too. Did you know, for example, that the average noise level in class-rooms is around 60 decibels, whereas recommended levels are no more than 35 decibels? One piece of research (Greenfield, 2007) found that the background noise of children's chatter, heating and lighting systems, fish tanks and computers meant that children were missing one word in six.

So a good place to talk will have good listening conditions for children. The Worcesterhire SLCN Pathway website (www.worcestershire.gov.uk/slcnpathway) has an excellent 'How acoustically friendly is your listening environment?' quiz, which you can use to score your setting and decide what actions might be needed to improve listening conditions.

It is worth auditing your environment at different times of the day, too, to see when noise levels peak. One early years setting found that the peak was at group snack time – a time when children might have good opportunities to chat, if they could only hear each other. In response to this finding, the setting arranged a rolling snack time, so that children could choose their own time and go to a small table and chairs with a tablecloth, fruit and drinks laid out.

The National Deaf Children's Society have provided really good guidance on how to manage noise in the environment, not just to benefit children with a hearing impairment but for all children (see their Acoustic Toolkit at www.ndcs.org.uk). They note that children will find it hard to listen if there is a lot of reverberation and echo, as in rooms with hard surfaces (large uncovered/painted walls, glass windows and tiled/wooden floors) and high ceilings. A second key factor is background noise that drowns out the voice children are trying to listen to. A good listening environment is where the signal to noise ratio is high (i.e. the sound level of the speaker is much higher than the background noise).

Adults are often able to understand speech even if background noise levels are louder than the speech signal. They can work out words that they have missed, due to background noise, if they have a good knowledge of words. They can then use this knowledge and 'bank' of words to make a guess at what the word would be. As children have learnt fewer words than adults, this task is harder for them. Similarly, the task will be harder for children of any age who have a limited vocabulary. Another factor is temporary hearing loss; at any one time point, one in six children have glue ear, and this is concentrated in younger age groups.

This means that young children and those with underdeveloped vocabularies require a positive signal-to-noise ratio to understand speech. The younger the child, the higher the signal-to-noise ratio needs to be. As adults, we should not assume that children can cope with noise just because we can.

To improve the listening environment, schools can try to reduce reverberation by fitting curtains or blinds, keeping blinds half closed rather than fully open, covering hard surfaces with fabric (for example, as a background to displays), installing special acoustic tiles, panels and door seals. Ways of reducing noise include closing doors, managing the timetable so as not to place noisier activities next door to quiet ones, getting those humming lights and noisy projectors and heating systems serviced regularly, sticking soft pads (or halves of old tennis balls) on the bottom of chair and table legs, carpeting as many areas as possible (to lessen noise from chairs), using soft covers on display tables, lining equipment trays with felt, and of course teaching children how to manage their own voice levels in class. I saw teachers make excellent use of:

- a consistent gesture, picture or sound (tinkling wind chimes are my favourite) for 'quiet';
- discussion to decide whether a task required no voices, whisper voices, partner voices, group voices or playground/breaktime voices; and
- visual indicators of noise levels in the shape of card or whiteboard 'noiseometers' (see the classroom management tools page on www.primaryresources.co.uk).

There are also commercial products to monitor noise, like Chatter Tracker, which uses a traffic light system. The teacher can pre-set the acceptable noise level, then as noise levels increase lights change from green to amber then red, with or without a siren sound. There is even an iPod 'Touch' and iPhone 'AudioTools' sound level meter traffic light app, which teachers and pupils can use to measure and manage sound levels in class.

Finally, if I could wave a magic wand to improve listening conditions in schools I would have Soundfield Systems installed everywhere. They consist of a radio or wireless microphone worn by the teacher and loudspeakers placed around the room. They present the teacher's voice at a consistent level around the classroom. Portable systems are available that can be moved between learning spaces as required.

Adult language

Early-years practitioners and teachers are hugely creative in thinking of resources and activities to stimulate language development. One thing I noticed, though, was that they often do not realise that they themselves are the best resource of all – that how they interact with children is the single biggest factor influencing how children actually *use* resources and take part in activities, and how far language will therefore be promoted. Adults who can adapt their language so it stimulates conversation form the most important part of a communication-friendly environment – a place to talk.

In Every Child a Talker, adults learned about the key interaction styles that promote language development. They learned, for example, that adults tend to interrupt children's activities by looming over them and asking a string of supposedly 'educative' questions like 'Do you know what that's called?', 'What colour is it?', 'Can you count them for me?' and 'Show me all the big ones'. Unfortunately, this style of interaction tends to produce one-word answers from the child, at best. As we saw in Chapter 2, a 'serve and return' mode where the adult tunes in sensitively to what the child is doing, thinking and saying will be much more helpful in promoting language development. Thus, instead of looming and questioning, the practitioner can get down to the child's level, watch, listen, wait and comment on what the child is doing. So, for example, 'Mmm ... my favourite ice cream is raspberry' would be better than 'What colour ice cream do you like?', and 'I liked the bit in the story where ...' would be better than 'Which bit did you like best?'. To help practitioners make the change in their interactions with children, Every Child a Talker had a useful visual reminder of the optimum ratio of comments to questions, called the 'hand rule' or 'five-finger rule' – four comments to every one question.

When practitioners do ask questions, these can be open rather than closed. If children say something incorrectly, they can avoid telling the child it was wrong but simply model back the correct version. They can take a child's language from one level to the next by reflecting back what children say in expanded form, and promote conversational interaction with peers as well as with the adult ('Why don't you ask your friend if they would like a cup of tea?', rather than 'Why don't you make me a cup of tea?'). A traffic light model (Figure 4.2) can be used to prompt this type of reflection and comment.

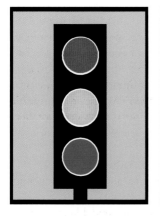

STOP/WAIT

Let the child lead the play and wait for them to lead the interaction

OBSERVE/LISTEN

Watch what the child is doing and note any attempts to communicate

RESPOND by modelling language that is useful to the child.
- Repeating back what the child says in correct form
- Expanding – repeating what the chid has said but adding one or two words
- Commenting – describing what the child is doing or looking at

Figure 4.2 **Traffic light model**

Exactly the same principles apply to interactions with older children. So, for example, if a child uses incorrect grammar, instead of correcting it the teacher can *reformulate* – take what the student has said and repeat it back in correct form – so 'She were going on at me' becomes 'OK, she was going on at you...'. They can *elaborate*, extending what the student has said – 'OK, she was going on at you, criticising you...' They can *comment* – 'OK, she was going on at you. I wonder what that was about?'

At all ages closed questions can be replaced by ones like these:

- What do you think would happen if...?
- I wonder...
- What do you think about...?
- How do you think we could...?
- Tell me about...
- How did you do that?
- How are you going to...?
- Perhaps...

Sharing books

Another context in which we often interrogate children or go into instructive mode is sharing books. We come, for example, to a picture of a tiger and say 'What's that? Look, he's got stripes. Do you know what he eats? He lives in the jungle.' I saw wonderful practice in Every Child a Talker settings, where practitioners had been trained to use dialogic book talk instead, to make the book corner a key place for talk.

In dialogic book talk, the adult shares a familiar book with an individual or group. In advance they think about comments they will make, open-ended questions to ask and key vocabulary introduced in the book. Table 4.1 shows a possible planning sheet. Such book talk is followed by planned opportunities for children to apply new learning. For example, after sharing 'Goldilocks and the three bears' one to one with a child and discussing what we eat for breakfast, a practitioner might add some cereal packets to the role play area so that the new vocabulary can be used in a meaningful context.

Taking stock of your environment

A number of useful tools are available to help you audit your setting, to assess the extent to which it provides a good place for talk. For the early years I recommend the Every Child a Talker audit described earlier in this chapter (available from http://earlylearning consultancy.co.uk/resources) and Worcestershire's early years setting audit for a communication-friendly environment (www.worcestershire.gov.uk/slcnpathway). These tools enable practitioners to take a comprehensive look at their environment, but for a quick snapshot, here are a few key questions I have found useful:

- How much background noise is there – what could be done to reduce it?
- Are real and toy objects – like story sacks and puppets – used to support story reading, and are they available for children to retell the story afterwards?
- Are there role-play areas inside and outside? Do adults use them to model language?
- Are there quiet listening areas (e.g. to listen to story tapes)?

Table 4.1 Dialogic book talk

Book title:	
Prompts and open-ended questions e.g. I wonder why… I wonder what the bear is thinking… I wonder what will happen when he gets home…	Prompts and comments inviting the child to relate the book to their own experience e.g. I don't think I'd like a bear under my stairs… When I was little I was scared of…
• _____ • _____ • _____ • _____ • _____	• _____ • _____ • _____ • _____ • _____
Key vocabulary	Follow up experiences to consolidate new vocabulary e.g. Relevant small world figures or role play area props, so children can re-enact the story • _____ • _____ • _____
Golden rules: WAIT for the child to respond to your comments – don't jump in! Recast and expand what the child has said.	

- Are there quiet areas in which practitioners can spend one-to-one time with a child?
- Are there cosy, enclosed spaces?
- Does the book corner have a good stock of familiar books that children can re-read, so as to help them internalise the story vocabulary and language?
- Are there displays children will want to talk about?
- Is there equipment outside that encourages shared play?
- Do adults tune in to children, follow their lead and comment?
- Do they know how to repeat back what children have said in correct and expanded form, make questions open not closed, choose and model the vocabulary and language structures they want children to use?

For Key Stage 2 and secondary phases, Worcestershire also have on their SLCN Pathway website a very useful 'Whole-school audit for a communication-friendly environment', with sections on adult language, a visually supportive environment, a welcoming environment, a comfortable environment, managing seating, promoting independent learning, the use of adults, and teaching topic-related/key vocabulary, for example.

Finally, one brilliant idea I saw was having pupils themselves undertake an investigation into how communication-friendly the school environment is. At Over Hall primary school in Cheshire, for example, classroom research by a group of children showed that adults needed to use different styles of interaction, and children needed to get better at listening. This led to CPD (continuing professional development) for both parties! In secondary schools, interesting work has been done in which students measure background noise in classrooms (great for their science lessons), take photos, interview other pupils, gather views from surveys and present their results.

Summary

In this chapter we have looked at how to ensure that the environment in settings and schools fosters language development. But a place to talk is not enough in itself. Children and young people also need to have genuine, relevant reasons to learn use the more formal and disembedded language that helps them to succeed in school and in life. It is to this – a reason to talk – that we turn in the next chapter.

A place to talk

A sensory garden

A place for conversations

Source: © Elizabeth Jarman

A place for story talk

Source: © Elizabeth Jarman

A place for the imagination

A reason to talk

Introduction

While I was waiting in the 'green room' to be interviewed on Radio 4's *Today* programme about my role as Communication Champion, I was lucky enough to meet regular contributor Rabbi Lionel Blue. He told me this wonderful story about why some children might be late talkers:

> An Austrian couple have a son. After the birth, medical tests reveal that the child is normal. There is nothing to worry about. As the child grows older, he learns to do everything except talk. For some reason he never speaks. The concerned parents take him to the doctor, who reassures them that as the child is perfectly developed in all other areas, there is nothing to worry about and that he is sure the speech faculty will eventually blossom. Years pass. The child is five, and is still not speaking. The child's mother is especially distressed by this, but attempts to conceal her sadness. One day she makes soup for lunch. As the family sit at the dinner table, the child suddenly declares, 'Mother. This soup is a little tepid.' The parents are astonished. 'All these years,' the mother exclaims, 'we assumed you could not speak. And yet all along it appears you could. Why? Why did you never say anything before?' 'Because, mother,' answers the child, 'up until now, everything has been correct.'

This story underlines the point that children, and adults, talk for a purpose. There has to be a *reason* to make us communicate.

A reason to talk in the classroom

In most classrooms children have plenty of reason to use informal conversational language. Whatever they are supposed to be doing, they will chat about what was on telly last night, what Amy said to Sunita, what's happening at the weekend. The purpose is to exchange views, cement friendships and gather information that is of interest to them.

It is less common, however, for classroom learning to provide a reason for children to use the more extended and formal styles of talk that support learning. In most lessons, teacher talk dominates, interspersed with closed questions usually requiring pupils to give short answers. Research shows that that the ratio of closed to open questions is in the order of five to one in Key Stage 1 classrooms, and three to one in Key Stage 2 classrooms (Hardman *et al.*, 2001) and that the average length of a pupil's contribution to a class discussion is just four words (National Literacy Trust, 2011).

The questions we ask children, moreover, are almost always ones to which we already know the answers. Answering questions that are not really questions at all, and having what education guru Mick Waters calls 'false conversations' – what authentic reason to communicate does this offer children?

After the teacher talk and questioning part of the lesson, children generally go off to undertake solitary tasks. Even when seated in groups, as is common in primary classrooms, they are generally doing work that does not require collaboration and co-operation beyond minimal interactions like 'pass the rubber', or off-task conversational chat.

All this off-task talk, in turn, attracts criticism from the teacher. Children get a message that talk is undesirable and holds no value. In other words, as one teacher told her class, 'I don't mind if you co-operate, as long as I can't hear you.'

Contexts for talk

It doesn't always have to be like this. I have visited and heard about many schools and classrooms which give children real reasons to use talk, for a range of purposes. Classrooms where teachers talk less and children talk more. Classrooms where teachers do what a wise head teacher, writing in the *Times Educational Supplement*, suggests: 'Scrap the mechanistic reliance on hands-up, ask more open-ended questions (why? how?), give thinking time, make space for collaborative conversations and oral rehearsal of answers, and then always ask pupils – rather than us – to comment upon the answer they have just heard' (Barton, 2011). Classrooms where adults ask questions to which they don't already know the answers. Classrooms, moreover, where children 'do things for real' and are stimulated by their experience to *need* and *want* to talk.

Here is my top ten list of 'for real' contexts that provide a reason to talk:

1.   Surprise
2.   Children asking the questions
3.   Children giving instructions
4.   Collaborating
5.   Giving an opinion
6.   Debating
7.   Using technology
8.   Reminiscing
9.   Drama and role play
10. Philosophy for children

No Pens Day Wednesday

All my top ten contexts for purposeful talk featured strongly in schools which have chosen to take part in the Communication Trust's 'No Pens Day Wednesday', introduced in the national year of communication and now a regular fixture in the education calendar.

Here are some brilliant examples of what schools got up to on No Pens Day Wednesday.

CASE STUDY

At St Joseph's primary school in Camden, a time machine had arrived in the playground overnight. Covered in silver foil and cordoned off, it had a huge clock with backwards numbers, a 0–9 number pad, a *Blue Peter*-type control console and – best of all – a calendar with Wednesday 28 September marked with a cross and the words 'St Joseph's School, Earth' scrawled across the page.

The local community policewoman came down to check for health and safety, while the children came out in class groups to explore and talk about the machine. The oldest children discussed what year they might want to go back (or forward) to. One girl said 9/11, so that 'we could stop it happening'. A child in a younger class suggested that maybe if you pressed a number on the number pad you would become that age – 'You'd be six…or nine…'. Others speculated about where the machine might have come from – 'I think it came from the sky' and 'I think the teachers made it' – while the teachers encouraged speculative language and modelled exciting vocabulary.

Then each class used the time machine as a stimulus for no-pens activities. In Reception the creative areas had been set out with foil and glitter and boxes for the children to use. Older groups discussed, planned and made their own robots and time machines in design and technology.

In Year 6 children imagined fast-forwarding to the future in a time machine. The children took part in an extended improvisation about life in the year 3011. One activity was group work to plan a talking brochure for a school in this new world. They had to choose a name for their school and its vision statement, then use their bodies to create a still image for the front cover of the prospectus. Later they recorded the images using camera and sound, and went on to work on the inside pages.

CASE STUDY

At All Saints school in Oldham, No Pens Day was a mixture of 'normal' lessons adapted to be speaking- and listening-based, and games and discussions about the importance of effective communication. When Year 6 came in they found a mysterious sign saying 'Press me!', with an arrow to a button on which their teacher had recorded a short message explaining what No Pens Day was all about. They listened to the recording and had a discussion about what it would be like to learn all day without pens, and what the pleasures and problems might be. They then had a ten-minute challenge to see if they could learn a non-verbal form of communication (some signs from British Sign Language). In literacy, rather than write about their favourite genre, author and book the children were challenged to come up with a radio or TV presentation to advertise it. In maths, they completed a carousel of problem-solving activities without pens. In the afternoon they played Chinese whispers and discussed how easily messages can become distorted, then improvised characters arriving at a party while their friends had to guess who the characters were. The day ended with a debate. The class had been thinking about a new breed of micro-pigs, and after reading several different articles on the subject they took positions on the question 'Micro-pigs – cool or cruel?' and justified their views.

CASE STUDY

At Coppetts Wood primary in Barnet, No Pens Day started with a whole-school assembly introducing the 'Pen Police' – six Year 6 pupils in uniforms, who asked every class to bring their pens and pencils to the hall so they could be locked up. Throughout the day they roamed about, checking that no one was using a pen. At the end of the day there was a mock trial of anyone caught out – mostly members of staff. The police presented their case against each defendant and they had a chance to plead theirs. The judge (another Year 6 pupil) asked questions then gave his verdict. He found them all guilty and handed out some harsh punishments including, for one teacher, scraping her class's plates in the dining hall.

CASE STUDY

No Pens Day proved to be a huge success at Frizington community primary school in Cumbria, where children had the opportunity to be history detectives, looking at World War II mysteries in groups. They analysed a bag of evidence, hypothesised, and presented possible reasons and answers to the class. Staff were also barred from using pens throughout the day and so classes came up with inventive ways of taking the register using stickers, stamps or finger prints next to their name.

CASE STUDY

At a secondary school in Leeds, a Year 8 maths set were given a challenge – to get the most chocolate. Different numbers of bars of chocolate were placed on three tables. Students then chose which table they wanted to go to (in secret). They then sat round their chosen bars of chocolate and worked out how many pieces each member of the group could have. This always turned out to be unfair on some. They repeated the process, discussing strategies as they began to 'see' the problem more clearly. All the pupils enjoyed the activity; one boy got so interested he even invented a new-sized bar to guarantee every student the same amount.

A science lesson started with a matching activity where pupils worked in pairs to match pictures of specialist cells with their names and how they are adapted to their function. Pupils then worked in small groups from diagrams and instruction sheets to make models of cells using salt dough, plastic bags, string and jelly. They took photos of the cells they had made, next to the name and diagram of the cell. They had a list of words that named the structures in the cell that they had to use in their talk to each other, and then they were asked to explain what each part of their model was in the real cell, using these words. The students really enjoyed the activity, staying in voluntarily at lunchtime to finish their models and clear up the mess. One student said it was the best science lesson she had ever had in her life.

Surprise

Surprise makes human beings want to talk – to exclaim, check out with others what might be happening, explore ideas about the event and so on.

Schools often use this element of surprise to launch a new curriculum topic. Head teacher Chris Fenton (2012) describes how he uses the unusual and unexpected in his teaching.

> A lot of my humanities planning starts with the phrase *The children walk into my classroom and . . .* They might, for example, find glitter (space dust) everywhere and charcoal scrapings in the shape of a spaceship landing on a desk, with a note in a plastic cylinder from Zog, claiming that his planet was much better than earth (more unusual animals, better weather and more amazing landscapes) and challenging the class to prove him wrong.

Steve Eddison, who teaches at Arbourthorne primary in Sheffield and writes regularly for the TES, is another master of surprise. He describes, for example, how his Year 3 class were transfixed by a large cardboard box with the words 'DANGER. DO NOT DISTURB' written in big red letters on the side. The class had just been reading *Where the Wild Things Are* and were soon speculating that there might be a wild thing in the box. A letter then 'arrived' to confirm this, and Steve was able to suggest that persuasive letters inviting the creature to a wild rumpus might lure him out of his box. The end of this story involved Steve in holding the box lid down as it tried to open, and a huge glove puppet hidden inside the box jumping out to a crescendo of screams.

At a school in Brighton, as a stimulus for No Pens Day activities, staff had hidden artefacts in the sandpit so children could explore Roman archaeology. In Newark, teachers disguised as aliens arrived at a whole-school assembly and took all the children's pens, because 'you write too much'. They did give them back at the end of the day! And when a Year 2 class at Waterville primary, North Shields, who were working on traditional tales, tried to get into their classroom after play, they found the door to the playground locked. Their teacher told them she was worried that a stranger had been in the classroom – dark-haired with a pale, pale skin. Making their way in via the inside door they found a table set for eight. There was much discussion. Who could it be? Why eight places? The children soon worked out that Snow White must have been involved. In turn, groups used the area for role play, requesting extra props such as apples and a mirror and taking the parts of different characters.

Another example of the use of surprise comes from a Year 2 lesson observed in St Thomas of Canterbury primary school in Salford.

> The lesson was part of a cross-curricular topic on dinosaurs. The teacher had earlier 'planted' a dinosaur egg in the classroom. The pupils were convinced that it had arrived through the roof. This captured their interest straightaway. . . The pupils had become very protective of the egg and made a nest and prehistoric forest for it to live in.
>
> Early in the lesson observed, the classroom assistant entered to announce that the dinosaur egg was missing. Genuine consternation: 'What shall we do? Has it hatched out? When did we last see it?'. Pupils were sent to investigate the disappearance. The class talked about it and agreed that the police should be contacted. How should we describe it; size, texture, colour and so on? One pupil was chosen and used the teacher's mobile phone to call the policewoman (actually a friend of the teacher). The policewoman arrived, interviewed the pupils but then got called away. She asked the pupils to complete

a crime sheet and said that she would return later to collect it. The teacher arranged the pupils into small groups, all with a team leader dressed in a police helmet and fluorescent jacket, to investigate and prepare the report.

What was particularly impressive about the lesson was the effective use of literacy skills in 'real-life' contexts ... It was important for the pupils to get things right so that the policewoman could be accurately briefed over the telephone. So it mattered what time the egg went missing, what it looked like, and what evidence about its disappearance could be supplied.

(Ofsted, 2011b)

Children asking the questions

All too often, adults are the only ones asking questions in classrooms.

At West Thornton Primary in Croydon, part of a 'Developing Talk for Learning' initiative (Croydon Local Authority, 2012) staff noticed how difficult their Reception children initially found it to ask questions. 'The class was very confused and could not grasp the idea of questioning at all, saying statements and delivering pieces of information instead of trying to find out something new', wrote their teacher. Observation showed that teacher talk dominated – 'I had chatted away merrily for twenty minutes and asked eight questions. The children had not attempted any.' Over the next few weeks, the class teacher and teaching assistant took on various roles and modelled questions children could ask to find out more about the character. They provided starters (who, where, why, what, when, do you ... ?) and collected questions on the whiteboard under these headings. Children became characters of their choice, using hot-seating and puppets. Their classmates were now able to put questions to them, using the models they had heard.

The next observation showed a significant change. The class were learning about the Chinese New Year, and this time had no difficulty in working with their talk partners to generate questions to ask Nia the dragon. The teacher's role was now one of listener and scribe.

Beginning work on a new topic is a good point to encourage children's use of questioning. Teachers can ask children to identify what they already know (recorded as a giant mind map) – and to frame questions about the things they would like to know. In plenaries, too, students can question each other about their work or be asked to jot down one question they will ask at the start of the next lesson to check the class have remembered the key learning (not activity) from the previous lesson.

Children giving instructions and providing descriptions

Barrier games are a very good way of giving children a reason to talk, and a reason to listen. In a barrier game, a screen or large book is placed between two players. Often the partners each have identical equipment in front of them. One player gives verbal instructions to the second, who must listen and respond to the instructions. They can ask for clarification or to add more detail. At the end of the activity the barrier is removed and the pupils discuss the outcome.

Examples might be:

- One partner giving the other instructions on how to find treasure on a map.

- One partner making a Duplo model and then giving their partner instructions on how to make exactly the same model.
- Each child having a set of picture cards showing Victorian toys. One child chooses a card and describes it; the other child has to pick the card that matches the description.

The rule for both children is 'Don't look'. The rules for the instructor are 'Give clear instructions or a description. Wait.' The rule for the follower is 'Listen carefully. Ask a question if you are not sure.'

Barrier games are very effective in promoting the 'formal talk' we touched on in Chapter 1, because the presence of the barrier removes the context from the interaction. They are also a good way of helping children understand how to ask questions to seek clarification if they have not understood what was said to them – an essential classroom and life skill, as we shall see in Chapter 6.

There are great ideas for barrier games in ICAN's *Communication Cookbook* (www.ican.org.uk), in the Talking Partners intervention programme which originated in Bradford (www.educationworks.org.uk) and on the websites of national EMA networks (such as www.emaonline.org.uk) and local authority EMA services such as Milton Keynes (www.milton-keynes.gov.uk/emass).

Collaborating

Collaborative pair or group work is an ideal way of providing a reason to talk. Many teachers are familiar with ways of structuring group discussion and interaction such as talk partners, turn-and-talk, think-pair-share, triad teams, snowball, envoying and jigsaw.

The use of talk partners (where pairs of children are given a short time to come up with an answer to a question, or to share their opinions) is common in primary schools, where it fits well with 'carpet time'. It is less often used in secondary classrooms, though I saw some teachers use turn-and-talk, in which pupils in one row turn round to talk to the pupil behind them. Many schools I met were finding that for more extended discussion, trios (sometimes called triad teams) proved more effective than pairs or larger groups – small enough so all are involved, but big enough to have people to bounce ideas off. Trios worked best where they included a higher, middle and lower attaining child and where adults modelled how to exchange ideas. One teacher, for example, would make a point of joining a group where one member was absent.

Think-pair-share allows a pair of children to join another pair; snowball allows for fours to become eights, and so on. In both these techniques, children share their partner's ideas as well as their own. In the envoy technique, children work in groups on a task, then one person from each group is selected as an 'envoy'. The envoy moves to a new group to share their group's ideas or findings and to find out what the other group discussed or achieved. They then report back to their original group. A brilliant idea I saw used at Elizabeth Garrett Anderson was choosing envoys by giving them a card looking like a travel pass (an Oyster card, in this London school) saying 'You will be a travelling envoy. When your group have completed the task you must move to the next group to your right in order to . . .'

In the jigsaw technique, children belong to two groups – a 'home' group and an 'expert' group. Each person in the home group is assigned a number, then all those in the class given a particular number (such as three) re-group to form an expert group. As experts, they research and become familiar with one aspect of a topic. If the class are studying rivers, for example, there might be expert groups looking at the water cycle, the use of rivers for transport, their use to generate energy, their use in farming, and their use as a focus for leisure opportunities. If the topic is Henry VIII, each expert group might find information about one of Henry VIII's wives. Once they have researched their topic, children return to their 'home' group to pool their knowledge

Giving an opinion

Everyone likes to give an opinion, and I saw some really good ways of enabling pupils to give theirs. 'Pupil voice' initiatives such as School Councils and Parliaments are an obvious example, as long as they do not just involve those pupils who are already highly articulate.

One school I visited used the idea of Antony Gormley's Trafalgar Square 'One and other' event to set up its own plinth in school, which children and staff used to make a speech about something that the felt strongly about. In Sheffield, schools could buy a wooden 'soap box' from the local authority, for children to use. The initiative culminated in a 'Speakers' Corner' event in the centre of town.

One of the interesting organisations I came across as Communication Champion was the Speakers' Corner Trust, a charity that helps young people from all backgrounds become 'speakers', able to express their views, engage in public debate and be active citizens. The charity can provide school-based workshops for students. It has also collaborated with others to develop a website (www.youthamplified.com). The resources on the site focus on confidence, listening, projection, persuasion, negotiation and argumentation and include:

- animated films in which young people discuss the skills they need to speak confidently and effectively in public;
- videos in which young people talk about speaking challenges they have faced;
- a self-evaluation quiz to identify personal speaking strengths and weaknesses;
- a guide designed to help teachers and youth workers support young people in the development of these skills across the curriculum and outside school.

Speak Out, an initiative from another charitable organisation called the Speaker's Trust, also provides really useful workshops for young people on public speaking skills, and organises challenge events for schools.

Debating

Debating is not just an archaic activity beloved of more traditional government ministers. If we can give young people lots of practice in debating skills – particularly those who are socially disadvantaged – we immediately help them move confidently into the more formal language of which they may have little previous experience. We also help them build confidence.

I was reminded of this when listening to a former director of children's services describing taking a party of pupils to take part in a European debating competition in which they competed with public school students. 'Our pupils were very bright,' he said, 'but as soon as they got onto the stage they crumpled up. They are sharp . . . they have the wit, the intelligence . . . but what they don't have is the ability to translate that into language.'

There is evidence (Akerman and Neale, 2011) that debating activities can have a positive effect on attainment. Research conducted in urban American high schools showed that students who took part in debating activities were 25 per cent more likely to complete their formal education than those who did not. Debate was also associated with improved literacy skills and subject knowledge in science, history and art.

I saw really interesting debates on local and national issues, with topics such as 'How far should you go to stand up for what you believe?' and 'Do video computer games affect your brain?'

In one Year 6 class, Ofsted (2011b) observed pupils applied their debating skills in a court-room scenario, role-playing a courtroom scene in which a jury has to decide whether to ban fox hunting. The class had been researching facts and drafting short arguments, which they presented to the court. The lesson showed pupils attempting formal language, avoiding abbre-viations and slang as they stated their views. The teacher moved into role, consulting with the jury before the verdict was announced. Near the end of the lesson, pupils put on different types of 'thinking hat' to review the issues raised. They then planned the next steps: 'We could write letters to people. In maths, we could do voting.' Pupils were keeping journalists' note-books to record what they thought, knew and wanted to find out. When the lesson ended, they were still talking about what they had been doing and what to do next.

There are several organisations which support the development of debating in schools. Debating Matters (www.debatingmatters.com) specialises in sixth formers, but has topical resources relevant to younger pupils too. Debate Mate (www.debatemate.com) works in primary and secondary schools. It is an international educational charity dedicated to improv-ing social mobility using cost-effective peer-to-peer debate mentoring. It trains undergraduates from top universities to run weekly after-school debating clubs in areas of social disadvantage. The charity also provides bespoke workshops for teachers looking to inte-grate debating into their classroom, and specialised training for students who want to 'debate like a world champion'.

Independent evaluation of Debate Mate's work showed that two thirds of students who took part enjoyed classroom discussions more than before, and 85% said they had become more confident and articulate. Pupils showed an average increase of two Speaking and Listening national curriculum levels over a period of 15 weeks. Debate Mate's work has been praised by Ofsted:

> Supported by mentors from the university, students engage in speaking and listening games but also practise debating skills. Topics include things such as: 'should voting be compulsory?' and 'should the monarchy be abolished?' In addition to debates within school, there are competitions across London and opportunities to work with competi-tion winners from other cities. Boys are very keen on Debate Mate. They see it as being particularly helpful in relation to future careers, 'It'll look good on my CV...I want to be a lawyer and it will be very helpful.' Students agree that the sessions are fun, that they have given them confidence and that they also help to develop their listening skills. They enjoy the occasional political discussions and talks and many of the boys like the compet-itive nature of the events. These skills are then complemented by oral work, drama and debates in mainstream English lessons. All this goes some way to explaining why boys do so well in English.
>
> (Ofsted, 2011b)

Using technology

Recording devices

Putting a microphone or any other recording device into children's hands instantly challenges them to generate decontextualised talk. It gives a purpose to the activity, and helps develop a sense of audience.

It need not be technologically complex. I watched groups of three-year-olds confidently using Easispeak microphones to record speech, play it back and delete it when they had finished. I saw slightly older children use the microphones to be 'roving reporters', to share songs and rhymes, to tell and retell stories, downloading and saving their recordings as WAV or MP3 files.

There are numerous other devices that can record brief pieces of speech and link this to images. Examples include talking tins, talking buttons, tell-a-story cards, recordable speech bubbles, think/say/feel recordable cards (shaped like a speech bubble/thought cloud/heart), talking photo albums, talking postcards, and sound shuffle sequencers. Pie Corbett's recordable story mountain, for example, is an A5 wipeable postcard which enables children to record a ten second message to support the main five aspects of narrative: the opening (once upon a time), the build-up (one day), the problem (unfortunately), resolution (luckily) and the ending (finally).

A number of suppliers stock these recordable devices; TTS (www.tts-group.co.uk) has a particularly comprehensive catalogue. They are being used increasingly and creatively in schools, for example, to enable children to:

- record instructions for a game or process;
- sequence pictures and tell their story;
- prepare input for assemblies;
- prepare talking captions for a display;
- develop talking mindmaps about a topic; and
- develop a quiz for classmates to complete.

The devices can also be used to promote home-school links. Children or adults can record descriptions of events at home, to share at school – or vice versa. Parents of children learning EAL can be asked to record a question or statement in the home language using recordable photo albums with pictures of the child doing everyday activities.

In one special school, pupils used TalkingPENs to create an instruction board with a series of recorded oral instructions on how to play a game. These pens allow audio recordings to be transferred to 'hotspots' on a printed surface. In this case the students recorded the instructions on sticky labels fixed to photographs the students had taken of themselves playing each stage of the game.

In another school, children used a recordable bar/story sequencer to create their own spoken account of a visit they had made to a castle. The sequencer is a simple recording device made of clear Perspex with a velcro strip across the front for attaching cards that can display words, pictures or symbols. Children can record a ten second message to correspond with each picture (in this case, photographs from the visit) and then press a button for playback.

When I visited at Frederick Bird Primary in Coventry school I saw Talking Tins used on a display about the school's success in a recent city-wide debating competition. There were photographs of the debating 'team' next to the Tins on which they had recorded their memories of the competition.

School radio and podcasting

Another inspiring use of sound recording is the development of school radio stations, like the one at Lyndhurst primary school (see case study below).

CASE STUDY

At Lyndhurst primary school in Grove Lane, London, Grove FM broadcasts to the whole school every Friday with content generated by pupils. Programmes are based on the curriculum or any other issues that the children feel strongly about. There is also a school vimeo channel (http://vimeo.com). Year 5 and 6 pupils can attend an after-school radio club where they learn how to edit, write, research, direct and work as a team. They have also worked with real live radio journalists on questions and interview techniques.

A term's programming might include, for example, 'a brilliant chicken joke from Nursery', a story written by a pupil after studying Greek myths, facts about the Olympics, an account of a class trip, opinions on religion, the word in the playground about a royal wedding, anti-bullying raps written by the children, a broadcast by the School Council, an infomercial about computer hacking, and a special programme about transition made by Year 6 pupils who are preparing to go to secondary school and children who have left Lyndhurst in the last few years.

If a school radio station seems too big an enterprise, podcasting offers an alternative. I saw this put to particularly good use in a school where pupils make podcasts for other pupils, such as a geography investigation undertaken in Year 9 to be offered to the next year group.

There are many sources of podcasting advice and resources for schools, but one I came across was the not-for-profit Radio in Schools podcasting platform (www.radioinschools.co.uk), which enables schools, teachers, pupils and parents to create and share podcasts online. Podcasts are produced with the easy to use Virtual Studio, which is accessible anytime, wherever there is an internet connection. It's a really simple process with no need to download and install software, provides space for users to store files and operates in an e-safe environment. Content can be shared with the whole podcasting community via schools' individual home pages. The organisation also provides learning activities directly linked to the National Curriculum.

Software

Software that promotes talk and gives it purpose is developing rapidly. One good example is Crazy Talk, which allows children to script and give a voice to photos and images, animating them as if they were speaking the children's words. A photo is uploaded into the application and with some minor pinpointing of key elements of the image it can be brought to life to 'say' pre-recorded messages using automated lip syncing. Celebrities can 'announce' outrageous gossip and reveal plot lines; sports stars can change their teams or decide on new career paths and animated characters can reflect real life stories. Adventurous students have been known to upload an image of their teacher to allow an early home time, no homework and free play all day...

Another interesting use of technology for older pupils (who must be over thirteen to use the site) is the Xtranormal website (www.xtranormal.com), which creates simple animated movies in which characters 'speak' a script that pupils have written, using text-to-speech technology. It can be used to motivate children to create short pieces of dialogue, a news report, an explanation of a concept, or a short debate. The finished videos are hosted on the Xtranormal website or can be uploaded into blogs/VLE or YouTube.

Skype and video conferencing

Skype and video conferencing offer further opportunities for purposeful talk. The Skype in the classroom website has safeguards built into the privacy settings which make it suitable for classroom use. At Lent Rise Combined School in Buckinghamshire, Reception children's first Skype conference is with Father Christmas; older children have conversations with staff from major museums and even NASA. Many schools have developed international Skype partnerships with other schools. At Hamilton Community College in Leicester, students studying citizenship chat with classes at a Kentucky school about the latest political and economic developments in their countries. Special schools can team up with local mainstream schools, too, with pupils interviewing each other, asking questions about uniforms, lessons, meals, hobbies and interests.

The potential Skype holds for enriching learning in the humanities and sciences is obvious. What may need to be developed is teachers' skills in using the medium to explicitly develop specific language skills too – how to ask questions, for example, or the active listening skill of seek clarification if you haven't understood something.

Reminiscing

As we saw in Chapter 2, reminiscing about shared past events is an important way in which children develop their language skills.

Early-years practitioners are very good at making pictorial records of children's activities as a basis for shared talk. But while such books may be made in primary and secondary classes, they tend to be used for writing rather than shared reminiscence – yet sharing the memories (of school trips, for example) could be a wonderful activity for 'talk volunteers' from the community to undertake with a small group.

Drama and role play

Most primary teachers, though rather fewer secondary teachers (other than English teachers), will be familiar with the repertoire of drama strategies that can be used across the curriculum to support learning and develop talk – from puppets to hot seating, thought tracking, conscience alley, forum theatre and mantle of the expert.

A lovely example of the use of drama is given by English teacher Fran Hill, who uses 'group therapy' to deepen pupils' understanding of characters in the class novel, play or poem. Pupils work in teams of five or six, with one taking the role of one of the characters. They respond to questions from the 'therapists', such as what happened in your childhood to make you act as you do.

Ofsted (2011a) describe wonderful work at St Paul's academy in Greenwich, where in one lesson students applied their knowledge of TV programmes such as the *Jeremy Kyle Show* to J. B. Priestley's *An Inspector Calls*. Characters from the play appeared in turn, to be grilled by the presenter. The pupils work combined good understanding of the play alongside very good dramatic ability. 'Mr Birling' revealed all his characteristic pugnacity, arguing with the presenter: 'I don't appreciate you insulting my daughter . . . remember that life is hard', before storming out of the 'studio' exclaiming that 'I've got better things to do with my time.' The class booed and hissed, as appropriate.

Another example of the use of drama is work in Southwark, where with the help of drama consultant Nina Birch, and teachers who trained at local theatres to become Drama Champions, thirteen primary schools took part in a year-long project to develop children's oral language skills for writing. Children made puppets, used role play, re-enacted scenes and events, took guided tours, drew story maps and went on large story walks. They also saw their teachers and class helpers pretend to be characters from stories or periods of history. Over the year, they wrote a story based on two best friends, Misery Guts and Cheerful Chappie, broadly based on *Misery Moo* by Jeanne Willis. 'I liked it when my teacher was the miserable old cow. It made me laugh', said one child. Then the children made really disgusting cakes (spiders, maggots and cobwebs) and wrote recipes based on the Jeanne Willis book *The Rascally Cake* ('I loved the disgusting things; I didn't know all those disgusting words before', reported one girl). Head teachers noted at the end of the project that 'it has been truly inclusive, with all children inspired and motivated to achieve', that the quality of children's speaking and listening had improved, and that Key Stage 1 writing results had improved sharply as a result.

The website www.dramaresource.com has descriptions of commonly used and other less well known drama strategies, plus fabulous units of work and lesson plans for *The Gruffalo* (Julia Donaldson), *Funnybones* (Janet and Allan Ahlberg), and the topic of World War II evacuees. Similarly, *Shakespeare for All Ages and Stages*, a booklet from the DfE archive, provides a brilliant range of practical drama activities which can be applied well beyond the Shakespearean context itself.

Philosophy for children

Philosophy for children (P4C) is a classroom approach that develops children's ability to listen, explore, question and reflect through dialogue (www.sapere.org.uk). Children are presented with an initial stimulus, which might be a picture, a piece of film, or a text. They then come up with questions they would like to discuss, based on the stimulus. The class vote on the question they would most like to discuss as a group, and one question is chosen – as an example, this might be 'Should you always tell the truth?', or 'Is heaven the same for everybody?'

During P4C sessions children lead the discussion; the teacher acts as a facilitator. Children learn to listen actively to one another, to think before they speak, and give reasons for what they say.

I heard a wonderful example of the power of philosophical discussion in a Sheffield school serving an area of social deprivation. The teacher had read a Year 6 class the story of a scorpion who asked a frog to carry him across the river because he couldn't swim. The frog said 'Yes, if you don't sting me.' Halfway across the river, however, the scorpion stung the frog. The frog said 'Why did you do that? Now we are both going to die.' But the scorpion said 'I can't help myself. It's in my nature.' The children were asked to discuss the story, in small groups. One group drew a parallel with recent history – 'It's like 9/11 . . . it's like suicide bombers.' Another likened the scorpion to Judas Iscariot. Groups presented their ideas to the rest of the class, then held a class discussion on the question 'Are you responsible for your own actions?'.

Another lovely example of P4C in action is a primary class who used Michael Rosen's book *Sad* and several photographs depicting people looking sad as the stimuli. The children formulated the following questions:

- Do people like to be on their own when they are sad?
- What is sadness?
- Why do people cry?
- Is it alright to be sad?
- Why do people feel depressed?

They decided to focus on the question 'Is it alright to be sad?' and pursued this line of enquiry. They agreed that it was alright to feel sad and that sometimes as humans we could not control this. They developed a line of thought that suggested that there were times in a person's life when they felt greater degrees of sadness and that people should show how they feel, so that they can be helped.

There is some good evidence of the impact of P4C. Studies in Clackmannanshire with 10- to 12-year-olds showed significant improvements in cognitive abilities (average increase of 6.5 IQ points), self-esteem and confidence – and in classroom behaviour.

Summary

In this chapter we have explored classroom activities that provide real reasons for children to seek to communicate effectively. Together with the environments and supportive adult inter-actions that make for a good place to talk, they provide the foundations for language learning. Left to themselves, however, children and young people may simply use all these contexts to recycle what they already know about language. To take their skills to the next level, they will need something more than opportunities and reasons for talk. They will need explicit teach-ing strategies that target vocabulary, listening skills, sentence structures and the skills of social interaction. It is to these we now turn, in the next chapter.

A reason to talk: role play areas

Early Years Foundation Stage: garage

Key Stage 2: a 1940s living room

Key Stage 2: World War II Anderson shelter

Key Stage 2: an underground station

6 Teaching talk

Introduction

Providing children with an authentic reason to talk is a great start, but, as we have seen, it needs to be complemented by approaches which scaffold language and actively teach component skills.

Take circle time as an example. It can be an excellent way of giving children a reason to talk, and encouraging quieter children to participate through the use of games and rounds. It has also, however, been criticised as a language-learning opportunity because it does not allow for dialogue between the teacher and the individual pupil. The teacher may not comment on or expand what the child has said, or ask the question that takes them to a higher level of thinking. Teacher–pupil dialogic talk may be absent. So as well as the *opportunity* provided by the circle, it might be necessary to build in teacher response and also think about the scaffolding provided by sentence starters for rounds – 'If I were a . . . I would . . .' – to scaffold the language of the hypothetical, for example. It might also be necessary for the teacher to introduce and model new vocabulary for the children to use.

In this chapter I describe some of the most effective approaches I saw to actively *teach* language skills in ways like this. Evidence suggests that these will be helpful to *all* children's learning, but particularly important for those whose out-of-school experiences give them little exposure to reasoned discussion.

Building vocabulary

> The child who tells us 'In the book the writer says . . .' will do less well than the one who knows how to say 'In the novel the author suggests . . .'. These are the key words of our subject – novel, play, dramatist, suggests, proposes, implies – so let's display them and teach them much more explicitly.
>
> (Geoff Barton, head teacher at King Edward VI school, Bury St Edmunds, September 2011)

A key piece of learning for me in my role as Communication Champion (which, incidentally, neither my training or experience as a teacher and educational psychologist ever taught me) was the critical role which vocabulary size and depth plays in children's learning.

Vocabulary breadth refers to the number of words that have some level of meaning for us; vocabulary depth means the richness of knowledge that we have for words that we know. There is some evidence that depth rather than breadth is the strongest predictor of reading comprehension.

We should never assume that children know the meaning of even simple words. As a former educational psychologist, I assessed many children of all ages using a test that asked them to say what 'on purpose' meant. Very few could do this, despite often hearing 'You did that on purpose' at home and in school. Similarly, work with young offenders has shown that they often don't understand very basic words like 'victim', 'punishment', 'appointment'.

Maths vocabulary is particularly tricky, especially when words have a real-life meaning that is different from their mathematical meaning. 'Take away' might be a pizza, for example, and 'tables' something you sit at. One teacher recounted how, when she introduced the word 'prism', a child in the class immediately put her hand up to say 'My Dad's been in one of those'! Science presents similar difficulties when everyday words have different meanings in a technical context – think of 'agent', and 'uniform'.

Children start school with very different vocabulary size and depth, and starting with poor vocabulary has a cumulative effect. Andrew Biemiller, an expert on vocabulary learning, estimates that while the average primary-aged child learns new root words (words like 'rock' from which related meanings – rocking, rocky and so on – can be derived by adding prefixes and suffixes) at a rate of about 1000 a year, the 25 per cent of children with the poorest vocabularies acquire roughly 400 fewer root meanings each year than their average peers (Biemiller, 2011). The statistics are truly frightening. If a child is in the lowest 20 per cent in vocabulary knowledge at age five, and you want them to move to an average level within three years, they would have to learn *20 new words a day, every day, for each of those three years.*

An analogy I owe to Robert Robinson, School Development Consultant in Blackburn with Darwen, helps explain why this happens. Robert uses a metaphor of a football net. If you have a good net of words when you start school, you can easily catch all the new words you will learn – just by hearing them. If you have many holes in your net you won't be able to pick up the vocabulary from a language rich environment. It will have to be explicitly taught to you.

As we saw in Chapter 1, children who experience social disadvantage are much more at risk of starting school with a limited vocabulary than better-off children. Hart and Risley (2003) found that three year olds in higher socio-economic status families had vocabularies five times larger than children in lower socio-economic status families. Other American studies have found that disadvantaged and linguistically 'poor' first-graders (aged six) knew 5000 words, whereas linguistically 'rich' first graders knew 20,000 words. The differences are marked for secondary aged pupils, too; in a study in England which compared students from schools serving disadvantaged areas with students from more affluent areas on standardised language tests, the biggest differences were in vocabulary. US research (Beck *et al.*, 2002) shows that senior (Grade 12) high school students near the top of their class knew about four times as many words as their lower performing classmates.

Because of the 'football net' effect, children who start school with poor vocabulary find it harder to pick up words from context. This can apply to EAL learners, too – though not if they are secure in their first language, so that they have the conceptual web in which to place new English words, and not if schools make efforts to provide bilingual resources and involve bilingual adults in the classroom so that the child can make the link between the English word and their first language 'net'.

The cumulative deficit caused by starting off with a poorly developed vocabulary intensifies if children then go on to be struggling or reluctant readers. Encountering a new word repeatedly when reading independently is a prime way in which children's vocabulary develops as they grow older; one study (Nagy *et al.*, 1987) calculated that a typical 10- to

11-year-old could learn around 800 to 1000 words a year from their independent reading. Even if they do not have reading difficulties, having a low vocabulary can trap children in a vicious circle; they cannot read more advanced texts, so miss out on opportunities to extend their vocabulary.

The effects of 'ordinary' schooling

There is some worrying US research (Biemiller, 2007) showing that a year of being in Kindergarten, Grade 1 or Grade 2 typically adds nothing to a child's vocabulary – that teachers were better at teaching children to read words than to understand them. Cassels and Johnstone (1985) found that pupils had little understanding of important vocabulary (words like incident, component, random, negligible) and that this persisted throughout their school years. If they did not understand the word to start with, they still wouldn't understand it several years later.

Why does this happen? It happens partly because we may not realise that children don't know words that seem to us basic. Teachers may be aware that they need explain subject-specific technical vocabulary, but not know that they need to teach non-specialist vocabulary that recurs across learning contexts. We know from research, too, that teachers typically introduce a new word and explain it just once (Scott *et al.*, 2003), whereas children need to hear a word around six times (more if they have language difficulties) in a range of contexts that help them internalise its meaning, if they are to remember it.

Effective approaches to use in school

I came across excellent ways of changing normal classroom practice – ways of clarifying what vocabulary should be actively taught, and ways of teaching it so that it will be remembered.

First of these is deciding what vocabulary to teach. These ideas come from speech and language therapists Stephen Parsons and Anna Branagan, who have built on work in the US by Isabel Beck (Beck *et al.*, 2002) to devise a training programme for schools on an approach they have called STAR (select, teach, apply, review). They have now written a book about this approach (*Word Aware: A Whole School Approach for Developing Spoken and Written Vocabulary*, published by Speechmark) which I thoroughly recommend. In their programme, teachers are asked to identify the 'Goldilocks' words for the topic they are teaching – words that are not too easy and not too hard, but 'just right'. These will be useful words that children will use again in other contexts, rather than everyday words or words children won't meet outside the topic. Table 6.1 gives some examples.

Table 6.1 Goldilocks words from Victorian England topic

Too easy – words children will be using in everyday conversation and will generally pick up incidentally, without specific teaching, unless they have speech, language and communication difficulties	**Goldilocks words** – useful beyond the immediate topic and should be systematically taught and reviewed These will be words that are in the average adult's vocabulary.	**Too hard** – topic-specific words that just need explaining. The average adult may not have an in-depth knowledge of these words
toys	petticoat	gruel
children	hoop	workhouse

Other important Goldilocks words will be those abstract words that are used across the curriculum, and often in exams – words like 'describe', 'compare', 'evaluate', 'conclusion'. Staff then teach these Goldilocks words systematically on the basis of their sounds, their meaning, the words they go with and their links to the child's own experience. Teaching is multi-sensory – acting a word out or thinking of a consistent gestures for the word (like mopping your brow for 'weather'), and using songs or raps to aid recall. It might include agreeing a student-friendly definition of the word (not looking it up in a dictionary). An example from Beck's work is 'benevolent': while a dictionary definition might be 'characterised by expressing goodwill or kindly feelings; desiring to help others; charitable; intended for benefits rather than profit', this is of little help to children. They might come up instead with the more useful definition: 'a person who is happy and kind and does things to make other people happy and kind too'.

Teachers might also increase vocabulary depth by exploring differences between the Goldilocks word and similar words (the difference between 'benevolent' and 'generous', for example, or between 'steal' and 'seize' – both mean taking something that is not yours, but seize implies the use of force). The teacher can generate examples and non-examples ('If the man patted the child's head and gave him a coin, would that be benevolent? If he just smiled at the child, would that be benevolent?'). Linking to the child's own experiences is a particularly important step – 'Have you ever known anyone who was benevolent? What was it about them that makes you think so?'.

Once words have been taught, they can be Blu-tacked onto the back of a door at child height so children can pull them off to use in their writing. This means that they have opportunities to apply, their new learning. The words taught are regularly reviewed at increasing intervals – at the end of the lesson, a week later, at the end of the half term, the next term and so on. A simple way of doing this is to have a Word Pot from which child or teacher can pull out cards of the words which have been taught and give a definition. Teachers can give a definition and ask if it is true or false, have children complete a quiz about the words, or ask children to tell a partner what they know about the word. Homework can also be involved, and might for example include writing the word on a sticker that says 'Talk to me about...'.

Evaluation of this approach in Worcestershire schools proved that words taught using these strategies were recalled; children could later on explain what they meant. Words taught in the normal classroom way (introducing the word and explaining it just once) were recalled much less easily.

A web of associations

I saw another good way of ensuring systematic vocabulary teaching across a school at St Mary's, a special school in Sussex. Here the school's network has a set of interactive white board (IWB) slides (visual organisers) for all staff to use to teach new vocabulary. The system (Figure 6.1) aims to build a rich web of associations and is based on the ways we encode new words in our brains, using semantic (meaning), syntactic (grammar), phonological (sounds), orthographic (writing) and motor (speech) routes. So there is a slide (phonological) to enter the word and note with the children's help what it begins with, rhymes with, ends with and how many syllables it has. The next slide (semantic) maps where you would find it/what you do with it/what category it is in/what it looks like/how it feels. Then there is a 'words that go with it' slide; teachers link the new words with things the children already know. For example, they might say 'Triangle: do you know any other words beginning with "tri"? What do you think "tri"

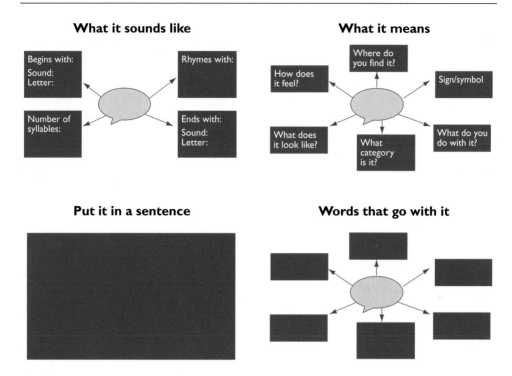

Figure 6.1 Teaching vocabulary

means?'. Finally there is a space for children to put the word in a sentence (syntactic route). All the learning is multi-sensory. Children write the word, say it, see it and hear it.

Another idea (Stahl and Nagy, 2006) is a 'four-square' semantic map (Table 6.2), which children complete following discussion, and the use of semantic feature analysis (Table 6.3). Research has shown that students who were taught using these techniques made greater gains in vocabulary knowledge than those who simply worked on word definitions (Bos and Anders, 1990; Nash and Snowling, 2006). Steele and Mills (2011) also suggest the use of Venn diagrams (Figure 6.2) to identify how two words may overlap in meaning but also may be distinct, and Mary Hartshorne at ICAN has a lovely example of 'word scales', like the one in Figure 6.3.

Table 6.2 Four-square semantic mapping

Target word nutritious	**Examples** Grapes Apples Bread Eggs
Student-generated definition Foods that are good for you	**Non-examples** Chips Chocolate bars Crisps

Table 6.3 Semantic feature analysis

	Lives in trees	Lives on ground	Makes nests	Uses tools	Lives in groups
gibbon	yes				
chimpanzee	yes	yes	yes	yes	yes
gorilla		yes	yes	yes	yes
orang-utan	yes		yes		

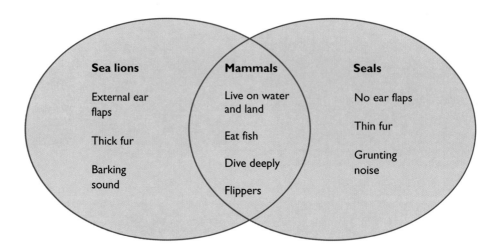

Figure 6.2 Semantic feature analysis – Venn diagram

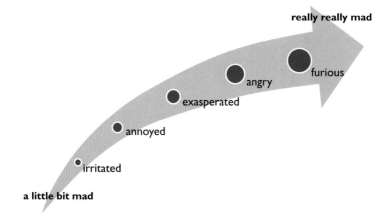

Figure 6.3 Word scales

All of these ideas use visual support to deepen understanding of important vocabulary. Visuals can also be used to make words more memorable – presenting subject vocabulary graphically, as in the examples in Figure 6.4.

Present words graphically

In geography lay out river feature words from source to delta...

Figure 6.4 Examples of visuals to make words more memorable
Source: Bristol SENCO newsletter, Spring 2011

Other great ideas which use visual support, in combination with 'Goldilocks words', come from the work of specialist teacher Pip St John. Pre-teaching vocabulary (PTV) is a free downloadable resource (www.widgit.com or www.tes.co.uk/teaching-resources) that gives children practical tools for independent word learning. The resource consists of prompt cards supported by Communicate in Print 2 symbols, which encourage children to think about the different features of a word, tapping into their semantic, phonological and perceptual word knowledge – what the word means, sounds like and looks like. Adults model how to learn the new words, either for the whole class or for small groups. The activities can also be given to parents as a talking homework task. The PTV prompt cards are presented in different formats; A4 for use on the wall, A5 on a washing line or small strips for use in the games. An A4 'how we learn new words' learning wheel/mat as a prompt for adults is also provided. The resources are very helpful for support staff to use to pre-teach key vocabulary to a child or group before the class begin to work on that topic. Again, this work has been evaluated and shown to make a significant difference to children's retention of taught words.

Teaching vocabulary may need to be a frequent and intensive classroom activity, for some children at least. The PTV and STAR approaches, both of which involve a relatively light touch, were both found to have a significant effect on the vocabulary that was actually taught, but not on children's scores on a more general vocabulary test. Beck and her colleagues in America, however, did find a significant increase in scores on standardised tests of vocabulary and reading comprehension for classes of ten year olds following five months of daily, thirty-minute vocabulary instruction that focused on learning in-depth word meanings, compared to a control group who received traditional text-book currricular instruction.

More ideas for teaching vocabulary

Table 6.4, taken from the former Key Stage 3 National Strategy resources, is a very useful resource for secondary subject teachers, giving them a range of different ways of developing pupils' vocabulary. Here are some other ideas I came across:

- Continuing to read aloud daily to children who are not reading independently themselves, in school and at home, using books with many unfamiliar words and discussing their meanings, and reading the same book two or three times.
- Using new and interesting words yourself, in the classroom – for example, instead of telling a student that they didn't quite close the door, say that they left it ajar.
- Explicitly teaching children word-learning strategies, such as using context and word parts to work out the meaning.
- Bringing explanations of words to life by using the interactive whiteboard to show pictures and video clips.
- Pulling key words from a display down onto the whiteboard at relevant moments, so that they are not just a static list.
- Having students complete a vocabulary grid of 'amber' words ('I'm not quite sure what this word means') and 'red' words ('I've never heard of this word ') when reading, so that the class or group can work on those words later.
- Using a student-friendly dictionary like *Collins COBUILD Advanced Dictionary*, which defines word meanings in accessible language.
- Using a quiz – give two incorrect and one correct definitions of a word and ask students to vote for the definition they think is correct.
- Teaching important Latin and Greek stems like –ology (the study of), which never existed as root words but combine with others to form meanings.
- Building a wow-word wall in the corridor, where children can add interesting new words once they can give their meanings.
- Having fun at www.wordle.net, which generates shapes and patterns from words. Ask pupils to come up with as many different words as they can that mean the same thing (words for 'very big', for example), and enter them into Wordle, where the patterns produced will give greater prominence to words that are more commonly used.

Teaching listening skills

After how to build vocabulary, the second most important knowledge for teachers in my view is how to teach listening skills.

What do you think your pupils would say if you asked them 'What do you do when you listen?' They would probably just say that you have to sit still. Like pupils, most teachers also tend to assume that listening is a passive process and children automatically know how to listen. One of the most interesting things I learned in my role was that both of these are myths. Listening, as experts like Maggie Johnson have taught us, is an active skill, and one that can be taught.

Listening skills develop over time, too. Every speech and language therapist knows the stages in the development of listening and attention described many years ago by Joan Reynell (Table 6.5), but many early-years practitioners would benefit from this information, as would many teachers of older age groups who have children in their class who are still at the earlier stages of being able to control their attention.

Table 6.4 Vocabulary activities for secondary subject teachers

1. Write key words on the board as they are used	2. Personal word books in which pupils record words as they are introduced to them
3. Highlighted key words in work sheets, notes and text	4. 'Jigsaw cards' – pupils match words with definitions
5. Read through the list so that students hear the words and repeat them	6. 'Lucky Dip' – pupil picks a word and explains what they know about it
7. Displays in rooms of key words/word banks	8. Group words/concepts – the whole group arrange words and their definitions into themes and concepts
9. Making sentences – pupils make sentences using the words in the box to show their meanings	10. 'Just a minute' – pupils select a word from the box and talk for a minute about it
11. 'Guess my word' – pupil picks a word and talks about it without saying the word – rest of the group have to guess the word as quickly as possible	12. 'Draw my word' (a version of the game 'Pictionary') – individuals pick a word out of the box and draw it for the rest of the group in 30 seconds
13. Word search – with definitions	14. 'Word bingo' where the teacher reads out the definition and the pupils strike out the word on their cards
15. 'Blockbusters' – a version of the TV game in which pupils or teams compete against each other to cross a frame made up of initial letter, for which definitions of subject-specific vocabulary are given	16. Anagrams
17. Subject-specific dictionaries	18. Word banks of subject-specific words located on writing frames
19. Interactive glossaries – lists of subject-specific vocabulary to which pupils add definitions at the end of lessons in which words have been introduced	20. Crosswords
21. Calligram posters – visual representations of words that reflect their meaning	22. Pupils create mnemonics for subject-specific vocabulary
23. Icons alongside words – icons or symbols alongside subject-specific words	24. Word cluster posters
25. Cloze passages with subject-specific words omitted	

Source: Key Stage 3 Strategy: Literacy across the Curriculum – spelling and vocabulary

There are also many different *types* of listening. Children may need to be cued in to what is expected of them – is it appreciative listening (to music, or poetry for example), or critical listening (detecting bias, distinguishing between fact and opinion, preparing to agree or

Table 6.5 Stages in the development of attention and listening

Level 1 (0–1 year)	Extreme distractibility. Attention shifts from one object, person or event to another. Any new event, such as someone walking by, will immediately distract. Attention is involuntary and 'captured' by stimuli.
Level 2 (1–2 years)	Single-channelled attention. Can concentrate on a concrete task of their own choosing. Cannot tolerate (ignores) verbal or visual intervention from an adult. May appear obstinate or wilful, but in fact need to ignore extraneous stimuli in order to concentrate on the task in hand.
Level 3 (2–3 years)	Still single-channelled. Cannot attend to competing auditory and visual stimuli from different sources (e.g. listening to an adult's direction while playing). But, with an adult's help, they can shift their full attention to the speaker and then back to the game.
Level 4 (3–4 years)	Still alternates full attention between the speaker and the task. Now does this spontaneously, without the adult needing to focus and re-focus that attention.
Level 5 (4–5 years)	Attention is now two-channelled. The child understands verbal instructions related to the task without interrupting the activity to look at the speaker. Concentration span may still be short, but group instruction is possible.
Level 6 (5–6 years)	The final stage. Auditory, visual and manipulatory channels are fully integrated. Attention is well established and maintained. Gradually able to shut out unwanted, irrelevant information and concentrate only on the essential aspects.

Source: Joan Reynell

disagree, or summarise), or empathic listening (listening for the emotions behind the words and the speaker's intent)?

Each of these types of listening will have a different set of skills associated with it, such as connecting, checking, deciding on importance, inferring, predicting, questioning or synthesising.

Students can be taught specific listening strategies:

● Repeating an instruction to yourself – silent rehearsal.
● Identifying the key words in an instruction.
● Drawing mind maps to link ideas and words together.
● Saying if you did not understand.

I was struck by how important this last point – saying if you don't understand – is for learning, and saw many examples of teachers who took pains to create an 'asking' environment where children felt comfortable to ask for repetition or explanation. They did this by praising children who asked for clarification, giving children practice in deciding whether instructions or requests made sense, and modelling 'asking' language (Table 6.6).

I also saw teachers give children cards they could hold up to tell the teacher what they needed. Figure 6.5 shows an example, but children could also choose their own images from the web.

Table 6.6 Showing children how to ask if they have not understood

Communication breaks down because	What you can say
The other person speaks too fast	Please could you slow down a bit?
The other person speaks too quietly, or there is a lot of background noise	I'm sorry but I couldn't hear what you said. Could you say it again, please?
The other person uses unfamiliar vocabulary	I don't know what X means. Please could you explain?
The message is too long	Could you say it again please, it was a bit long for me to remember?
The message is unclear	Did you mean...?'

	Too fast	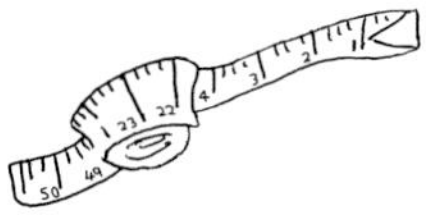	Too long
	Hard word		Too quiet
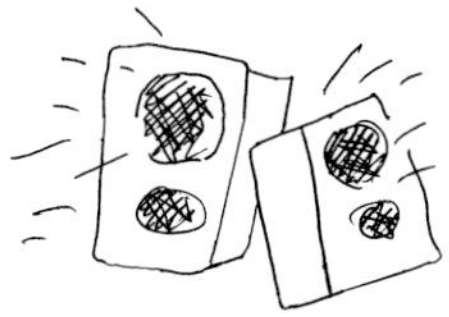	Too noisy		Too confusing

Figure 6.5 Ways of showing you haven't understood

A great activity from a resource called *Tactical Teaching: Speaking and Listening* (Bindon, 2006) is to give children specific listening roles such as:

- Build on – agree with and add to what you have listened to.
- Summarise – summarise what you have listened to.
- Compare it – compare what you have heard with other things you may have heard or read.
- Question it – ask a question to clarify or seek more detail.
- Disagree – 'I don't agree with what has been said because...'

The roles could be allocated within small group or whole class discussion. In whole class discussion, they could be combined with a useful technique called 'bouncing' (Gershon, 2012) in which the teacher takes what a pupil has said then asks another pupil to comment on it – 'Thank you for making that point, Jo. Andrew, what are your thoughts on what Jo just said?'. Teachers can extend this to 'Can you build on what Jo just said/summarise what she said/compare her ideas with Andrew's/decide whether you need to ask Jo for more detail/give reasons for agreeing or disagreeing?'

CASE STUDY

At Haverstock School, as part of a very successful project in a number of secondary schools in Camden and Islington, speech and language therapists have worked with teachers to develop a structured approach to teaching listening skills. Posters set out the key themes of looking, taking turns to talk, thinking, focusing and checking understanding. These are actively taught; for example, students are given specific ways of saying that they have not heard or understood something. Feedback from students has been very positive – 'I can work better in class because I have better understanding of what the teacher tells us'; 'If the teacher says a word that you don't know then you can ask – say "I don't understand that word"'.

There are several good resources which make it easy for teachers to develop listening skills. *Teaching Children to Listen*, by Liz Spooner and Jacqui Woodcock (Continuum Press, 2010) is a book packed with ideas to use with a whole primary class or with groups. It has training ideas for staff, and includes a straightforward way of evaluating each child's progress. Teachers are also given guidance on how to improve listening conditions for children, using the noise level audits described in Chapter 4 and changing seating arrangements so that during whole-class teaching children sit on chairs arranged in a horseshoe rather than the carpet. Local research has already shown that the approach makes a big difference in the classroom, reducing the numbers of children rated by their teachers as having severe listening and attention difficulties from 21 to 4 per cent in just six weeks.

Liz and Jacqui's model defines good listening behaviours as:

● Looking at the person who is talking.
● Sitting still.
● Staying quiet so that everyone can listen.
● Listening to ALL the words.

For each of these there are active games – like 'Is it me?' for listening to all the words ('If you are a boy and you are eight line up at the door'; 'If you are a girl with dark hair, put on your coat'), or for looking at the person who is talking, 'Who is the leader', where one child goes out of the room then comes back to guess who has been given the role of leading actions (clapping, tapping…) for others to follow.

Other excellent resources include *Learning to Listen to Learn*, by speech and language therapists Helen White and Christina Evans (2005), which has an easy-to-implement programme of two fun and interactive teaching sessions and a follow-up booster session to develop pupils' listening skills, with comprehensive facilitator instructions and all the resources needed for the sessions.

Teaching inference skills

A subset of listening skills are the skills of inference – working out the implicit meanings behind words.

> The ability to make inferences is, in simple terms, the ability to use two or more pieces of information in order to arrive at a third piece of information that is implicit. Inference can be as simple as associating the pronoun 'he' with a previously mentioned male person. Or, it can be as complex as understanding a subtle implicit message, conveyed through the choice of particular vocabulary by the writer and drawing on the reader's own background knowledge.
>
> (Kispal, 2008)

A good example of one common type of inference ('gap-filling') is the well-known poem by Ogden Nash.

> Algy met a bear.
> The bear met Algy.
> The bear was bulgy.
> The bulge was Algy

The poem does not state that the bear ate Algy – that is what has to be *inferred* from the listener's previous knowledge of bears' behaviour.

A useful resource for teaching inference skills is *Language for Thinking*, published by Speechmark (with training information on www.languageforthinking.co.uk). The resource can be used with small groups in the classroom. It is suitable for Year 1 and Year 2, and older primary children with SEN. It is based on fifty photocopiable picture and verbal scenarios with associated question sheets carefully structured to promote children's development of inference. A simple black and white picture scenario of a crowded bus, for instance, is presented to a group of four to six children. A brief story is read to the children and questions asked to promote discussion. Questions start with the concrete, such as 'Who is sitting down?', extending slightly to 'What might happen if the bus goes too fast?' before reaching the most abstract level questions such as 'Why might the old lady feel upset if she didn't get a seat?' The materials include prompts for further discussion and practical activities, as well as optional literacy activities.

Other than this resource, most of the work on inference I came across tended to be about reading rather than listening comprehension. This need not matter. A literature review (Kispal, 2008) by the National Foundation for Educational Research (NFER) identified strategies for teaching inference in a reading context, but there is no reason to believe they would not be appropriate for listening comprehension too. Indeed, the report suggests that one evidence-based strategy for improving reading comprehension is practising inferential questions on aurally presented texts: inferring 'can be practised outside the domain of reading with pupils of all ages', and 'one way of cultivating these skills in young readers and reluctant readers is to do it in discussion, orally.'

The strategies the NFER review suggests include:

- Teacher modelling – teachers 'thinking aloud' as they read aloud to pupils and asking themselves questions that show how they monitor their own comprehension.
- Teachers making explicit the thinking processes that result in drawing an inference.
- Teacher questioning: asking 'How do you know?' whenever an inference is generated in discussion of a text, asking questions about relationships between characters, goals and motivations, asking questions that foster comprehension monitoring, such as 'Is there information that doesn't agree with what I already know?'.
- Questioning by pupils: training pupils to ask themselves 'why' questions while reading; teaching the meaning of the question words 'who', 'when', 'why' and so on; asking pupils to generate their own questions from a text using these question words.
- Activation of prior knowledge: asking pupils to generate associations around a topic, and discuss and clarify their collective knowledge.
- Choosing the right texts: taking care not to choose texts that are too easy for classwork, since very explicit texts provide few opportunities for inferences to be made.

So, for the 'Algy met a bear' example, the teacher might think aloud ('I'm wondering what it means when it says the bulge was Algy. What do I know about bears? I know they sometimes attack people and eat them. So that's what it must mean – the bear ate poor Algy'), or activate prior knowledge by asking the children what they know about bears, or ask 'What do you think happened to Algy? How do you know?'.

The NFER report concludes that inference can be seen in children of all ages. It can be practised early on, with pre-readers, using picture books, but research indicates that pupils are most receptive to explicit teaching of inference skills in their early secondary years.

Teaching children to work in groups

Observing schools' responses to No Pens Day Wednesday, I was struck by the differences in children's ability to work together in groups. In some classrooms, they were able to listen to each other, build on one another's views, stay on track and reach a conclusion. In others they argued, cut across each other, meandered, split off into pairs to chat, or simply gave up – just like many adults in meetings!

The difference related to opportunities the children had previously been given to *learn* the skills of groupwork, and the *structures* they were given to support their talk – like the children in the case studies below.

CASE STUDY

At Gresham primary in Croydon, observations of a Year 6 class showed that children were able to use paired talk effectively. Then they were asked to share their ideas in a group:

> We noticed an immediate change...the quieter children stopped talking, some pairs still continued as pairs, children did not take turns and did not listen to each other. After ten minutes the children were getting frustrated and it was clear they were getting off task.

In the next lesson children were asked to think about what makes good group work. Each mixed ability group prepared a poster then presented their ideas to the class. Children recorded their thoughts about their own strengths in contributing to group work, and areas they could develop.

The posters were displayed and regularly referred to. After a few weeks, observations showed a marked improvement, with more turn taking and greater participation by the quieter children.

CASE STUDY

At St Paul's Academy in Greenwich, students were considering different features of a film text such as genre, audience and narrative. Groups were organised with roles allocated to students such as 'scribe' and 'expert'. At a given point, the experts moved around to present their ideas to a new group, their thoughts meticulously noted down by other students. In a third lesson, with a bottom set in Year 9, students were asked to debate the pros and cons of an issue related to the text they were studying. Roles were allocated in each small group, for example, 'speaker', 'summariser' and 'chair', and issues were formally debated. Students were fully engaged, listened carefully to each other and attempted to make use of the rhetorical devices that had been previously discussed (from Ofsted, 2011b).

There are many good ways of teaching children groupwork skills. The 'Getting on and falling out' theme materials from primary SEAL, for example (www.sealcommunity.org) systematically develop children's abilities in working with others, using the developmental framework of learning objectives proposed in the QCA/Primary National Strategy's guidance on teaching Speaking and Listening (Table 6.7).

The SEAL resources include checklists ('Working together self-review checklists') for different age groups, which can allow children to reflect on their developing skills. An example of one of the checklists is shown in Table 6.8.

The progression in the SEAL programme helps ensure that, in Ofsted's words, 'the group work is planned carefully and structured so that all students have a role and know what is expected of them. It does not become an opportunity for some students to sit quietly knowing that others will do all the talking' (Ofsted, 2011b).

Another very useful scheme for both primary and secondary schools is Cambridge University's successful 'Thinking Together' approach (http://thinkingtogether.educ.cam.ac.uk). Devised by Neil Mercer, the scheme teaches children how to hold a reasoned discussion, tackling problems through talk. It is based on over a decade of classroom-based research into the relationship between talking and thinking. Children are explicitly taught about exploratory talk and as a class agree on a set of ground rules for talking together. They then work in groups of three, using exploratory talk for curriculum-based activities. There are ideas for these activities on the website and in the team's books *Talk Box* (ages 6–8), *Thinking Together* (ages 8–11) and *Thinking Together in Geography* (ages 12–14).

The approach has been rigorously evaluated using experimental and control groups to enable comparisons to be made of the quality of children's talk in groups, the development of

Table 6.7 A progression in learning to work in groups

Year group	Group discussion and interaction
Foundation stage	Interact with others, negotiating plans and activities and taking turns in conversations
Year 1	Take turns to speak, listen to others' suggestions and talk about what they are going to do Ask and answer relevant questions, offer suggestions and take turns Explain their views to others in a small group, decide how to report the group's views to the class
Year 2	Ensure that everyone contributes, allocate tasks, consider alternatives and reach agreement Work effectively in groups by ensuring each group member takes a turn, challenging, supporting and moving on Listen to each other's views and preferences, agree the next steps to take and identify contributions by each group member
Year 3	Use talk to organise roles and action Actively include and respond to all members of the group
Year 4	Take different roles in groups and use the language appropriate to them, including the roles of leader, reporter, scribe and mentor Use time, resources and group members efficiently by distributing tasks, checking progress and making back-up plans
Year 5	Plan and manage a group task over time using different levels of planning Understand different ways to take the lead and support others in groups Understand the process of decision making
Year 6	Consider examples of conflict resolution, exploring the language used Understand and use a variety of ways to criticise constructively and respond to criticism
Year 6 progression into year 7	Adopt a range of roles in discussion, including acting as a spokesperson, and contribute in different ways such as promoting, opposing, exploring and questioning Identify and report the main points arising from discussion Acknowledge other people's views, justifying or modifying their own views in the light of what others say Work together logically and methodically to solve problems, make deductions, test and evaluate ideas.

their reasoning skills and their curriculum attainment, before and after the scheme was implemented. Results show that after around six months students engage more effectively with tasks for longer periods of time, with all participants being included more in discussions and an increase in reasoned discussion. The word 'why', for example, was four times more likely to be used in the experimental group than the control group. There were significant impacts on attainment in science and maths, and in non-verbal-reasoning.

Table 6.8 Working together example self-review checklist (Year 5/6)

Level	Question	How well did we do?		
All	Did everyone feel OK about being in the group?	Very well	So-so	Not very well
Year 5 Term 1	When you were planning, did you think about and plan how long the task might take overall, how many sessions you would need to complete it and so on, as well as thinking about what you needed to do straight away?	Very well	So-so	Not very well
Year 5 Term 2	When you needed to make a decision in the group, did you think about the consequences of each possibility?	Very well	So-so	Not very well
	Did you make sure everyone had a say?	Very well	So-so	Not very well
	Were you able to reach a compromise when people had different ideas?	Very well	So-so	Not very well
Year 5 Term 3	Did you have a leader of the group?	Very well	So-so	Not very well
	Did you agree what the leader of the group should do – for example, encouraging others and making sure that everyone has a turn and deciding what to do when people can't agree?	Very well	So-so	Not very well
Year 6 Term 1	If you did not understand something, did it feel OK to ask the person to explain again?	Very well	So-so	Not very well
	Did you say if you did not agree with something and did you have a chance to explain why?	Very well	So-so	Not very well
	If someone said they didn't agree with what someone else said or did, did that person ask them why and listen to their reasons?	Very well	So-so	Not very well
	Did it feel OK for people in the group to disagree?	Very well	So-so	Not very well
Year 6 Term 2	Did you use 'peaceful problem-solving' to try to find a win-win solution if people didn't agree in the group?	Very well	So-so	Not very well
	Did the language you used and the way people said things to each other make a good solution more likely?	Very well	So-so	Not very well
Year 6 Term 3	Were the language you used and the way people said things appropriate for working together in the classroom? Did it help everyone feel comfortable?	Very well	So-so	Not very well

---

An example of an activity used in Thinking Together – Magic Squares

In this lesson the task is to talk together in a group in order to agree a strategy for solving a magic square, in which each row, column and diagonal must add to the same number. Agreed ground rules for talk are displayed and each group uses 'Talk Cards' ('What do you think? Why do you think that? I agree because... I disagree because... Any more ideas to share? Do we all agree... or shall we talk some more?') as a prompt to support their discussion. At the end each group gives an example of a problem and explains their strategy for solving it. The class review how they organised their groups and arrived at solutions, and how they used the ground rules for talk.

Talk frames

Talk frames provide children with a scaffold of sentence starter or structure appropriate to the particular language purpose – recount, agree/disagree, justify and so on. Figure 6.6 lists some of these purposes; I am sure there are many more.

Teachers can use charts like the ones in Figure 6.6 and Table 6.9 when planning learning opportunities, to consider whether a breadth of purposes are covered, and which ones might be missing from their lessons. They can scaffold language for any given purpose by providing and modelling talk 'frames'.

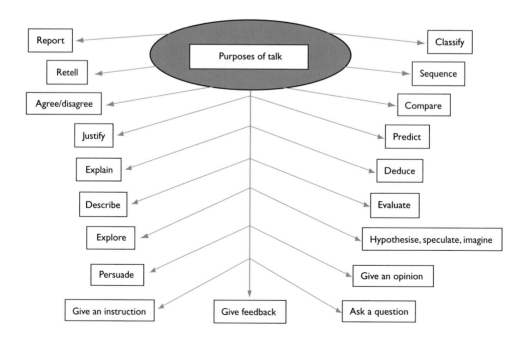

Figure 6.6 **Purposes of talk**

Table 6.9 Useful activities for developing talk

Purpose of talk	Teacher prompts	Example activity
Report	What happened?	Making a podcast news report
Retell	What happened first...next... finally?	Telling a familiar story to younger children
Agree/disagree	What do you think about what x said?	Class debates
Justify	What makes you think...how do you know?	Maths problems
Explain	Talk me through it...why do you think?	Review learning from a previous lesson by asking students to come to the front and talk the class through the concept
Describe	What could you say about?	Mock courtroom witness statements
Explore	What do we think...?	Philosophy for children discussions
Persuade	Convince me that...	Walk the line activity – children position themselves on a line to show where they stand on an agree/disagree continuum in relation to a statement (e.g. 'Eating animals is wrong') – they then pair up with someone from the opposite end of the line and have to put their point of view and try to persuade the other person to change their position – at the end of the exercise the walk the line activity is repeated
Give instructions	What do I need to do?	Barrier games
Give feedback	How was it, in your opinion?	Plenary sessions
Ask questions	What will you ask?	Hot seating, preparing a quiz for classmates to complete
Give an opinion	What do you think?	Soapbox activities
Hypothesise, speculate, imagine	What do you think might...?	Alternative endings for stories or films
Evaluate	What do you think of...?	Working with a partner to self-assess a piece of work
Deduce	What conclusions have you reached?	Be a detective – explore a bag of objects or a set of pictures
Predict	What might happen...	Science experiments
Compare	How are they similar/different?	Children choose two items from a topic related selection and say what is the same and different about the two things – record using Venn diagrams
Sequence	What comes first...next...?	Re-ordering paragraphs or pictures
Classify	Which go together?	Sorting objects, pictures, word cards

Many teachers are familiar with frames from their work on writing – 'first, next, finally…' for a recount, and so on. What is often forgotten, however, in this approach is that talk is not just a preparation for writing. It exists in its own right. In life and work we need to know how to give instructions, recount an event accurately, justify our ideas and so on *orally*. It is only in school that the assessment tail has wagged the dog and talk is seen as the bit part, not the main player.

Talk frames need to be age-appropriate. But what does 'age-appropriate' mean? What are the language structures we might model for a Reception class, a Year 1 class and so on? One of the most useful resources I saw in my time in as Communication Champion was a publication from the Tower Hamlets Ethnic Minority Achievement team, which provides guidance on what the progression might be, across the primary years.

The publication covers the purposeful use of spoken language to:

- agree and disagree;
- explain;
- compare;
- hypothesise;
- deduce;
- give an opinion;
- describe;
- predict;
- evaluate;
- retell;
- explain; and
- sequence.

For each of these, a progression is mapped from Reception to Year 6. Table 6.10 shows an example; the complete publication (*A Progression in Language Structures*) can be obtained from the Tower Hamlets Learning and Achievement Team.

Another very good resource for talk frames is Sue Palmer's *How to Teach Talk for Writing: Ages 8–10* and *How to Teach Talk for Writing: Ages 10–14* (available from www.suepalmer.co.uk). Originally designed to support writing, these cross-curricular materials are even more useful for helping children develop the more formal spoken language they need for learning. The photocopiable resources provide frames for individual, paired or group talk. They cover, for example, comparing, contrasting, giving evidence, stating or justifying an opinion (Key Stage 2) and giving examples, giving definitions, presenting opposing views (Key Stage 3). Children use the frames to prepare a spoken presentation; they then deliver the presentation and receive feedback. The books also include advice on progression, and assessment guidance.

One brilliant use of talk frames I came across was to help children reflect on the types of contribution they made in class discussion. Here, secondary aged pupils were given a set of coloured cards. Blue cards were used to express doubt or offer an alternative ('I'm not convinced that…', 'Yes, but on the other hand…', 'I wonder if…', 'Something else to consider is…'). Pink cards had starters which enabled the pupil to build on another person's contribution ('Thinking about what X said…', 'Going back to…', 'In that case…', 'Building on…'). Grey cards were used to ask for clarification ('I'm not sure I understand, please could…', 'So, are you saying that…?', 'Does this mean…?', 'Why do you think that?'). Finally, yellow cards were about offering one's own opinion ('In my opinion…',

Table 6.10 The language of argument – agreeing and disagreeing

Year group	Language structures
EYFS	He/she didn't share/take turns I want to …………………………… I like …………………………… I don't like ……………………….. I think …………………………… Why? I think …………………………… What do you think? I don't think ………………………… Why do you think this? It is …………………………… It's not ………………………….. Yes because ……………………. No because ……………………. I like …………………………… I don't like ……………………….
Year 1	Yes/no because ……………………. I like …….. because ……. and ……….. I don't like ……. because ……. and ….. I agree with ………….. because ……… It is right …………… It is wrong …………..
Year 2	No because ……………… Yes because …………….. I agree/disagree because ………. I think …… because …. and also because ……. However …….. Also ………….
Year 3	An argument for is ………. because ….. An argument against is ……. because ….. I understand however/due to/but/therefore ……… I accept your decision however I feel/believe …….. because/as/due/to ………
Year 4	An argument for …. is ….. because ….. and …. An argument against …. is …. because ….. and ….. I understand …. that …. depending on the content but would argue …. I understand your point of view, however I disagree because ……..
Year 5	In my opinion ……….. should be banned. I have two main reasons for believing this. First of all, as I'm sure you'll agree, … My second important reason for wanting to ban ……………. is that …………… Perhaps some people would argue that ……………………. that …………… However, I would point out that ………………………………………………….. It is clear that a ban on …………………………… would be a great step forward!
Year 6	On the one hand …………………………. but …………………………………… Convince me that ………………………………………………………………… I am convinced …………………………………………………………………… Given that ………………………………………………………………………..

Source: *A Progression in Language Structures*, available from Tower Hamlets Learning and Achievement Team, 3rd Floor Annexe, Mulberry Place, 5 Clove Crescent, London E14 2BG, Tel 020 7364 4677. Contact Tilly Nimako at Tilly.Nimako@towerhamlets.gov.uk.

'Unlike…', 'I disagree…', 'I partly disagree…'). As they made a contribution, pupils held up the relevant card, then put it to one side. At the end they could see whether they had a characteristic type of response. As a class, they were also able to reflect on whether any particular type of response was over- or under-used.

The need for practice using talk frames like these is underlined by research I came across (Bennett, 2003), showing the number of teenagers who have difficulty with using logical connectives which link together two propositions, such as 'moreover', 'consequently', or 'conversely'. Fewer than seven in ten 11- to 15-year-olds were able to use these connectives appropriately. They did better with the more commonly used connectives, which led the researchers to suggest that students' understanding of unfamiliar logical connectives would improve if they were exposed to them more frequently.

Talk for Writing

Although again badged (unhelpfully) as about writing rather than spoken language itself, Pie Corbett's wonderful 'Talk for Writing' approach (see the National Strategies Talk for Writing DVD pack) is brilliant for building vocabulary and sentence structures. In this approach, children work with a story or piece of non-fiction until they know it by heart and can perform it. Teachers are encouraged to teach (daily) a specific number of stories, poems or non-fiction texts per year, through communal and oral storytelling, using story maps and actions to help children remember key vocabulary. Initially the retelling should be communal and led by the teacher, leading to group story circles and then paired retelling of a story with children facing each other. Once the children have internalised patterns through memorable, meaningful repetition they can then use the 'storehouse' to create their own stories based on the ideas and structures learned orally.

Learning stories or non-fiction by heart in this way is a very powerful way of providing children with ready access to rich language which their everyday experience may not provide. For younger children, Bookstart's Rhyme Challenge and ICAN's Chatterbox Challenge provide similar opportunities to develop language structures by internalising rhymes learned by heart.

Social and emotional aspects of learning

Talk is not just about academic learning, 'cognitive' processes. It is also central to how we feel ('affective' processes) and how we relate to others – to social and emotional learning. The way we structure talk can support relationship building, or damage relationships; it can resolve conflicts, or exacerbate them. Children and young people can learn how to:

- Listen to others actively, in an empathic way.
- Ask open questions which encourage others to communicate.
- Communicate displeasure without blame, using 'I messages'.
- Give and receive feedback in ways that move learning on.
- Follow a communication rubric to resolve conflict.
- Use talk in teamwork in ways which help everyone contribute.

The National Strategies SEAL resources contain many activities to help develop these skills, particularly in the 'Getting on and falling out' primary theme, and the 'Learning to be together' theme in the secondary materials, which you can access at www.sealcommunity.org.

Below are some ideas for classroom activities, devised by SEAL expert Julie Casey.

Asking open questions

Ask the class to work in pairs, one pretending to be a celebrity of their choice and the other a journalist. The journalist has to come up with questions that will help readers feel they really know what the celebrity is like. Ask pairs to identify their best questions, and share these as a class. Draw out the differences between open and closed questions.

'I' messages

Give the class examples of things that might get said in an argument or conflict:

- 'You're always late – you're driving me mad.'
- 'How stupid was that – getting drunk and losing it?'
- 'You're so lazy – you never do your homework.'
- 'You've lost my top – I'm never lending you anything again.'

Ask what they would be likely to say in return. For each response, ask them whether it would cool or heat up the conflict. Explain that there is a special sort of statement that cools conflict, called an 'I message'. It has three parts:

- 'I feel...' (the feeling you get).
- 'When you...' (the action of the other person that is annoying you).
- 'Because...' (the effect on you or on the other person).

Give an example – instead of 'You're always late – you're driving me mad', the 'I message' might be 'I feel angry when you're late, because I have to hang around waiting for you', or 'I feel really worried when you're late because I'm scared something might have happened to you'. Ask the class to turn the other statements into 'I messages'.

Resolving conflict

Show the class an onion. Explain it has an outer tough skin. Peel it back to show the layers beneath.

Sometimes when two people or groups are in conflict it can be useful to peel back the layers and see what feelings lie underneath. Show an extract from a TV soap or tell a story about two characters are in conflict. Ask the class, working in pairs, to 'peel back the onion' and identify how each character was feeling.

Teach the SEAL peaceful problem-solving process:

- **Ready** (are you ready to think together?);
- **Steady** (take it in turns to talk about the problem and how you feel – use 'I messages', say what you need, think of solutions together, choose one idea that will work for both of you);
- **Go** (try out your idea);
- **Replay** (think about how you did it, and check if things are OK).

Tell the story of two sisters, quarrelling over who should have an orange. There was only one orange. Both said 'I must have that orange'. In the end after a long argument they cut the orange in half. One sister threw away the peel and ate the fruit. The other sister threw away the fruit and used the peel to make a cake. What can we learn from the story? Try out the peaceful problem-solving process, enacting the roles of the two sisters.

Giving feedback

Watch the film *Mean Girls*. Ask the group to identify 'put-downs' they hear the characters give each other. Ask pupils in pairs to talk about 'a put-down that really hurt me'. As a class discuss:

- Do we all use put-downs sometimes?
- Why is that?
- Do put-downs have the same effect on everybody?

Ask pupils to watch a programme like *The X Factor* and note down negative 'cheap laugh' feedback given by the judges. Collect some examples of these 'put-downs' and ask pupils to place themselves on an imaginary line on the floor to show where they stand – whether they think it is OK or not OK to use put-downs. They should talk to someone close to them in the line to exchange views, then to someone in a very different position on the line. Bring the class together and scribe the arguments for 'OK' and 'not OK'. Ask the class to come up with a list of 'pick-me-ups' (the opposite of put-downs) they most value from teachers, so they can share these in the form of a letter or poster for staff.

Teamwork

Ask pupils to make a short video on 'the worst group in the world'. The video should illustrate the behaviours that prevent effective groupwork, such as talking over each other, putting others' ideas down, and so on. Or ask pupils to come up with a set of rules for the worst group in the world (for example, everybody must talk at once, nobody must ever disagree with anyone else), then turn these on their head so as to create into a set of rules for effective group work.

Self-assessment and monitoring

An important aspect of all the 'teaching talking' approaches we have looked at in this chapter – whether it be teaching listening skills or how to work in groups – is making the learning explicit to children, and enabling them to assess their progress. I like the idea of using 'WMG' – 'What makes a good...' (e.g. member of a team) – to help the class become aware of what they are aiming at in their language learning. This is an example from Broadmead Primary school in Croydon:

> The class discussed WMG listening. We pulled out key listening behaviours, which included giving eye contact and staying quiet when someone is speaking. I used their ideas to make a poster to refer back to. I also introduced table signs that could be used by the children and other adults to reinforce the good listening skills. By talking about 'what makes a good listener' children were able to identify who in the class met the criteria. I

also modelled good listening to make the WMG explicit, and took photographs of the children who displayed the key listening skills.

(Croydon Local Authority, 2011)

Resources for teaching talking

In addition to the specific publications already mentioned in this chapter, I came across several general resources for teaching language. For 4- to 6-year-olds, ICAN's *Communication Cookbook* (www.ican.org.uk) is a resource book of activities focusing on essential ingredients that support children's communication skills in four areas – attention and listening, vocabulary, building sentences, storytelling and having conversations. There are four games for each area; most can be easily slotted into daily routines in the classroom or at home. The *Communication Cookbook* DVD, included with the book, demonstrates activities, top tips and information on ages and stages.

Another early-years and primary resource is *One Step at a Time* by Anne Locke (Network Educational Press). This is a programme that can be used without specialist training and systematically develops the skills of conversation (Nursery), listening (Reception), narrative (Year 1) and discussion (Year 2).

I Hear with My Little Ear 2, by Liz Baldwin (LDA, www.ldalearning.com), provides imaginative activities to develop key language skills in children aged 3 to 11, which can be fitted into PE lessons, circle times and spare moments in class.

Talk Across the Curriculum (www.educationworks.org.uk) is a cross-curricular reference guide and activity guide with over a hundred speaking and listening activities that can be delivered across all areas of the curriculum and for all ages from Reception to Year 8.

Communication in the Curriculum Language Packs (www.communicationitc.co.uk) are colourfully produced board games for groups of children, to promote language and communication development with children in Foundation stages and Key Stage 1, which link to common curriculum topics in geography, science and literacy. They are particularly useful for pre-tutoring: preparing children in advance for the vocabulary and concepts they will meet in the whole class situation. A bingo game, for example, relates to a Year 2 science unit of work on changing materials; children have baseboards describing features of living things, to which they match pictures, justifying the match ('I need this card because a horse has live babies.') The baseboards vary in difficulty (wings, four legs, swims, fur, feathers, scales versus wings, four legs, no legs, insect, has live babies, reptile).

For 14- to 19-year-olds, BT's *All Talk* DVD, workbook and website (www.bt.com/alltalk) is a fantastic free resource designed to be used in English lessons as stimulus material for discussion, role play and reflection. It simultaneously supports the study of spoken language for GCSE English language, and the development of pupils' own speaking and listening skills. The resource has 15 units, grouped into five contexts for communication and language – 'You talk', 'Offline/online talk', 'Street talk', 'School talk' and 'Public talk'. Here are some examples of the units:

- **Family talk over time** – This unit, part of 'You Talk', uses video clips and transcripts from TV soaps from the last 50 years – from *The Grove Family* to *Only Fools and Horses* and *The Royle Family*. Students compare the language used in the different periods then compile their own collection of conversations from recent soaps and sitcoms like *Coronation Street* and *The Kumars at Number Ten*.

- **Using talk in groups** – This unit has contrasting videos showing the same group of students planning a party together, more and less effectively. Students identify features of effective discussion and practise skills by, for example, working in groups to plan a flash-mob event. Follow-ups include watching Monty Python clips and *Vicar of Dibley* parish meetings, and exploring excerpts from literature like meetings in *Lord of the Flies*.

Another very useful resource for secondary pupils is BT's *Talk Gym*. It provides a tailored 'course' in communication skills based on an initial self-assessment. Students start with a Facebook app which asks them to rate their own skills (their talk fitness) by answering six questions about themselves, then nominate some friends or family to answer the same questions about them. Their answers appear anonymously in a graph. There is information on the communication skills needed for friendships, family, education and employment and practical exercises to build building strengths as a communicator – listening skills, being clear, group discussions and interview situations.

Finally, digitised spoken language collections are a good way to explore language. The British Library's Learning Playtimes website (www.bl.uk/playtimes), for example, has wonderful recordings and film footage of singing games, clapping songs, skipping rhymes and all kinds of imaginative play from over one hundred years of children's games. Or look at the archive of regional dialects and podcasts about the development of spoken English at the website of the British Library's 2010 Evolving English Exhibition (www.bl.uk/learning/langlit/index.html).

Teaching talk

Teaching vocabulary: a magpie wall of special words

Teaching vocabulary: choosing words all the adults will use

Adult language: using open-ended prompts

Teaching children how to work in groups

7 Support for talk

Introduction

So far in this book we have looked at how to create the right conditions for developing language and communication, by providing a place to talk and a reason to talk, and by teaching language skills to all children. This is not sufficient, however; we also need to support children in a variety of ways, identifying those who are struggling and planning strategies and interventions to help them.

Identifying children in need of help seems to work best if there is systematic tracking of where *all* children are in their language development, just as there is as for literacy and maths. In the early years, the Development Matters developmental grids (see Table 7.1 for an extract) provide a really helpful tool that simply involves 'colouring in' statements describing typical language development in broad and overlapping age bands. There are three headings – listening and attention, understanding, and speaking – with additional aspects of social communication covered in the personal, social and emotional development grids.

The Development Matters grids were based on the child monitoring profile used in the Every Child a Talker programme to enable practitioners to spot young children at risk of delay. Initial worries that this would be burdensome proved unfounded and the tool was enthusiastically welcomed by early-years practitioners, from childminders to Children's Centre staff.

The profile allowed settings to target extra help to those who need it, and carefully monitor the outcomes by tracking the child's progress on the profile's developmental scales.

Some local areas, like Sheffield and Worcestershire (www.worcestershire.gov.uk/cms/speech-language-communication.aspx) use an extension of the Every Child a Talker child monitoring profile into Key Stage 1 and 2.

Identifying children who need additional help

Better tracking for all children helps us get better at identifying those who need additional help. Research shows that many children with SLCN go unidentified. As we saw in Chapter 1, 65 per cent of young offenders were found by researchers to have SLCN, but in only 5 per cent of cases had this been previously known.

DfE 'PLASC' data also suggest possible problems in identification. Figure 7.1 shows a declining proportion of children identified by their schools as having lower-level SLCN as their primary need, as they move from Key Stage 1 to Key Stages 2, 3 and 4. At the same time, the proportion of children with specific or moderate learning difficulties, or behaviour difficulties identified as their primary need rises as we move up through the age groups. A speech

Table 7.1 Extract from Development Matters: communication and language – understanding

Birth to 11 months

- Stops and looks when hears own name.
- Starts to understand contextual clues (e.g. familiar gestures, words and sounds).

8–20 months

- Developing the ability to follow others' body language, including pointing and gesture.
- Responds to the different things said when in a familiar context with a special person (e.g. 'Where's Mummy?' 'Where's your nose?').
- Understanding of single words in context is developing, e.g. 'cup', 'milk', 'daddy'.

16–24 months

- Selects familiar objects by name and will go and find objects when asked, or identify objects from a group.
- Understands simple sentences (e.g. 'Throw the ball.').

22–36 months

- Identifies action words by pointing to the right picture (e.g. 'Who's jumping?').
- Understands more complex sentences (e.g. 'Put your toys away and then we'll read a book.').
- Understands 'who', 'what', 'where' in simple questions (e.g. 'Who's that/can? What's that? Where is?').
- Developing understanding of simple concepts (e.g. big/little).

30–50 months

- Understands use of objects (e.g. 'What do we use to cut things?').
- Shows understanding of prepositions such as 'under', 'on top', 'behind' by carrying out an action or selecting correct picture.
- Responds to simple instructions (e.g. to get or put away an object).
- Beginning to understand 'why' and 'how' questions.

40–60+ months

- Responds to instructions involving a two-part sequence.
- Understands humour (e.g. nonsense rhymes, jokes).
- Able to follow a story without pictures or props.
- Listens and responds to ideas expressed by others in conversation or discussion.

Early learning goal:
Children follow instructions involving several ideas or actions. They answer 'how' and 'why' questions about their experiences and in response to stories or events.

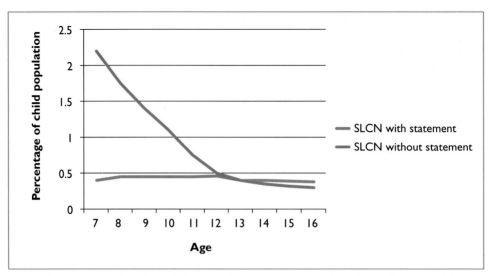

Figure 7.1 Percentage of child population with SLCN as primary SEN need type, from schools'
         PLASC return

Source: Adapted from a presentation by Professor Geoff Lindsay to NASEN conference, 2010

and language problem in Key Stage 1 'becomes' a literacy problem, a general learning problem, or a behaviour problem in subsequent key stages.

Some schools, like Beal High School in Redbridge (see case study below), have recognised
this and probe below the surface to better understand the needs of their intake. SENCOs
might want to consider following their lead and screening for SLCN whenever a pupil is
struggling with literacy, has BESD, or is at risk of exclusion.

CASE STUDY

Beal High School in Redbridge regularly has large numbers of children coming in at
Year 7 who have been identified by their primary school as having learning or behavioural needs. The school undertakes detailed work to identify any underlying SLCN that
might have been missed. Cognitive abilities tests (CATs) are used with all of the new
intake in September. Children with significantly lower verbal than non-verbal skills on
the CATs, or with low scores across the board, are targeted for further investigation via
round robins asking staff about their performance in class. As a result of training, subject
staff have become increasingly skilled in identifying potential SLCN. 'This child is not
remembering things . . . his sentence structure isn't right', they may note. As a next step,
the school may ask their speech and language therapist to assess and advise. As a result of
these systems, the large group of children with non-specific learning or behaviour difficulties has been reduced by the end of the first term, and specific difficulties – SLCN,
dyslexia, dyspraxia – identified so that appropriate interventions can be put in place.

There are many excellent screening tools that can be used to screen at-risk groups. Examples include the checklists in the Inclusion Development Programme (IDP) materials, the Afasic Checklists for children aged 4–10 in Jane Speake's *How to Identify and Support Children with Speech and Language Difficulties* (LDA), and the checklists featured in the Communication Trust's *Don't Get Me Wrong* publication. Table 7.2 draws on these and similar publications, and may be useful as a very quick guide for school-aged children.

There's much more information in a series of free booklets called 'Universally Speaking', available from www.thecommunicationtrust.org.uk. The booklets map language and communication development from birth to the teenage years, and suggest ways of finding out whether a child is or isn't able to do the things expected at their age.

For example, the early-years booklet suggests spending time with a four-year-old, to check out:

- Can they talk about events, explaining where they went and what happened? For example, 'Julie and Saria and me goed park and played on swings.'
- Can they use longer sentences joined up with words like 'because', 'or', 'and'? For example, 'I like ice cream because it makes my tongue shiver.'
- Are they easily understood by others?
- Are they able to follow simple two part instructions reasonably well? For example, 'Go and get me the big scissors and some blue paper from the drawer'.
- Are they able to understand simple 'why' questions about a story you have just read?
- Do they use talk to organise themselves and their play? You might hear them saying things like 'Let's pretend we are in a jungle, you be the … and I the …'.

Screening tests

Some schools and settings choose to supplement screening checklists with quick tests to substantiate practitioner judgements.

In the Blackburn with Darwen Reception project, for example, children are screened using the British Picture Vocabulary Scale (BPVS) and the Derbyshire Language Scheme Rapid Screening tool – a test of comprehension which involves children in following instructions of increasing length and information, using everyday objects.

Children starting school in September with a gap of more than one year between their vocabulary age and chronological age, or who are unable to follow instructions containing four key, information-carrying words, take part in a range of intervention programmes such as the Narrative programme (Black Sheep Press) and the locally developed 'Vocabulary Box'.

Children learning English as an additional language are screened in their home language. If this shows that any language delay is specific to English, the children may be offered the local authority's EAL Intensive Programme – 20 booklets of activities for teaching assistants to use with children who are at the early stages of learning English.

All children targeted for intervention are re-assessed on the BPVS and ratio gains are calculated to show their progress. This allows schools to evaluate the impact of their interventions, and also highlights any remaining language difficulty as the child moves into Year 1.

Other local areas use commercially available screening and assessment tools, such as SpeechLink, Language Link and WellComm to profile whole year groups.

WellComm covers the six months to six years age range and uses a 'traffic light' system to identify children requiring immediate intervention, as well as those who show potential

Table 7.2 Identification of SLCN

Understanding language – does the child:	
Have difficulty following long or complex instructions?	
Watch and copy others, because they have not understood an instruction?	
Seem unable to recount the events in a recent episode of a TV soap opera?	
Repeat what you say rather than responding appropriately 'What have you been reading?' – 'I've been reading'?	
Expressive language – does the child:	
Stammer or have an 'obvious' difficulty in saying certain sounds (e.g. 'pider' for 'spider', 'hostipal' for 'hospital')?	
Have difficulty with prepositions (under, over, behind, etc.) or tenses (ran, running, will run)?	
Use a lot of vague language, such as 'I dunno, it's kind of, something that's, well you know …'?	
Miss out words or put them in the wrong order?	
Struggle to retell a simple story or recount a sequence of events?	
Conversations and social use of language – does the child:	
Take metaphorical language literally – 'pull your socks up', 'it's raining cats and dogs'?	
Have difficulties understanding implied meaning – for example, interpreting 'Is your mother in?' to require a factual yes or no answer, rather than a request to go and fetch their mother?	
Talk about their own interests incessantly, not knowing when to take turns in conversation, or how to listen to somebody else?	

language difficulties. Screening is undertaken using a mixture of observation of the child, discussion with parents and direct testing. The resource provides intervention strategies to meet individual needs as identified through the screening process, and ideas for parents to use at home. It also provides reports that enable the school or setting to easily monitor and evaluate progress for individuals and whole year groups.

CASE STUDY

A number of settings in Warwickshire used WellComm to screen their children as part of their Every Child a Talker initiative. Children flagged up as 'red' could be immediately referred to the speech and language therapy service, while at the same time staff used ideas from The Big Book of Ideas which comes with the toolkit, to support them if there was a wait. Children at 'amber' took part in language enrichment groups and were then assessed again to check that they were making good progress. Staff valued the class reports that enabled them to group children with similar needs, as well as the ideas for individualised targets.

Devised by speech and language therapists, SpeechLink aims to help schools manage speech difficulties in children aged four to eight years. The computer-based screening tool takes less than 15 minutes per child to complete. It identifies children who should be prioritised for referral to a speech and language therapist and helps schools manage straightforward speech difficulties by implementing age-appropriate therapy programmes.

Infant Language Link is for children of four to eight years old, and assesses the child's understanding of spoken language. Results show which children need school-based language support (for which customised programmes are provided for schools, and parents), and which should be discussed with the speech and language therapy service. The assessment takes about 15 minutes to complete and involves the child choosing one of a set of pictures to match a spoken sentence. The customised pupil support plan identifies the level of support needed for each pupil assessed; it includes Wave 1 whole class strategies, differentiation strategies for identified areas of language, and detailed session plans for a four- to eight-week small group intervention programme. A real bonus are the reports which chart the levels of understanding of language for a whole class, enabling the school to identify the general receptive language levels of that year group. The recommendations in the whole-class profile enable the teacher to implement the necessary strategies within their class planning. Information on how to group particular pupils is also provided. Re-screening can offer supporting evidence of in-school improvement.

The Language Link team have worked with Cambridge University to standardise the assessment tool so that it gives scores against national norms. The data is also being used to evaluate the impact of the recommended interventions for children falling into the lowest 25 per cent of the range of language scores. Initial data is very positive, with children making 20 months progress on average after six months of intervention – 14 months more progress than the six months that would be expected through normal maturation (or eight months more after correcting statistically for what is called 'regression to the mean ', the normal tendency of children at the extremes of the any distribution of scores to move towards the middle over time).

CASE STUDY

Schools in Barking and Dagenham use Infant Language Link, with support from the local authority advisory team. Before it was introduced, the advisory team got lots of late referrals – such as children in Year 3 who often had EAL, whose teachers had waited to see whether the child was simply still mastering English. Language Link is used as a tool to help class teachers match the language they use to the needs of children in their class. A class profile, for example, might show that prepositions were a problem for many children in the class, so whole-class strategies would be needed. The teacher might put speech bubbles up around the classroom with the relevant words which every adult should make a point of using in their interactions with children. Staff would compete to see how often they could use these words.

Junior Language Link is a new development for 7- to 11-year-olds. It assesses receptive language and also the social uses of communication – understanding of sarcasm, making social inferences, starting and maintaining a conversation, interpreting facial expression, understanding the words that describe different emotions. The computer-based assessment (which includes the child watching and answering questions about a short video) takes about twenty minutes per child and can be used either individually or as a whole-class screen. Like Infant Language Link, it can provide reports for the whole class and for the individual, along with recommendations which enable the teacher to build the necessary strategies into their planning, and advice on setting up language nurture groups. Children's progress can be tracked by re-assessment, and progress demonstrated for parents and school inspection.

Secondary Language Link, for 11- to 16-year-olds, is the latest screening programme to be added to the series. It includes:

- an evaluation of pupils' understanding of language (concepts and complex instructions, sentences and short spoken passages), and
- a social understanding screener (recognising emotions and interpreting facial expressions, initiating and responding to conversation, and using language appropriate to the context – street versus classroom talk, for example).

The tool is again computer-based and highly user-friendly for teenagers. One example is an on-screen 'virtual classroom' which the student navigates in response to spoken instructions ('Put your maths book on my desk then sit at your desk', 'Log off your computer before you leave the class'). Another is a broadcast clip about a robbery, with questions to test whether the student can get the main idea, recall factual detail and make inferences. The social understanding screener has film of young people interacting, with questions to see if the student can read body language and identify appropriate and inappropriate styles of communication.

Supporting children with identified speech, language and communication needs

Having identified children with speech, language or communication needs, what can we do to help them? In this section I will describe some simple strategies for class and subject teachers – a basic toolkit that every teacher needs to understand.

The difficulties that these children have are varied. Some – like unclear speech, stammering or listening and attention problems – are obvious. Other children have more subtle difficulties such as restricted vocabulary, problems with grammar or with the social side of language. Hardest to spot can be children with receptive language difficulties. They struggle to follow instructions and are often one step behind the others, waiting to copy what they do. In reading, they may learn to decode well but not be able to answer simple questions about a book.

Why won't they listen?

Listening and attention problems are often seen as just a behaviour issue, but can reflect language difficulty or delay. As we saw in Chapter 6, there is a developmental sequence in learning to 'listen and do' at the same time, for example, and not every child will be at the same stage. Some will need you to say their name to get their attention, before you speak. Others will need to be asked to stop what they are doing to listen to an instruction. They will not be able to 'listen and do' at the same time.

Many children will need to be given more time to respond when you ask a question or give an instruction. Research shows teachers typically leave only one or two seconds between asking a question and expecting an answer. This allows the child barely enough time to process the question, never mind respond. It helps to use the 'ten second rule' (Figure 7.2), counting silently to ten. If at the end of this a time the child doesn't respond, try once more using the same words. If at this stage you rephrase in different language you are adding to the information-processing load and sending the child right back to the start of the process. Only if after this the child doesn't respond should you rephrase an instruction in simpler language, or scaffold the answer to a question with prompts.

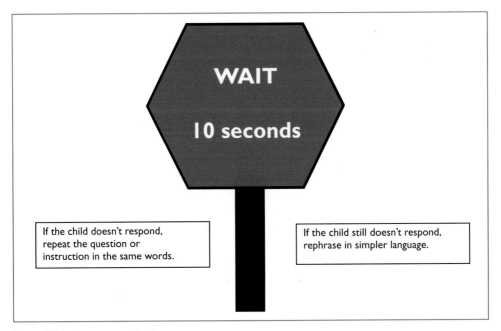

Figure 7.2 The ten second rule

A simple strategy like this can make an enormous difference. I remember well hearing about one boy who attended a school involved which had had training in how to give children more thinking time before expecting them to answer questions. He said 'I always felt stupid because I couldn't answer any questions in class. Now I can.'

Using visual support

A good exercise to help you support children with additional needs in language (one I owe to speech and language therapist Rebecca Bergmann) is to imagine yourself on holiday, in a foreign country. You can't yet understand any of the language and go into a restaurant to try to buy dinner. The waiter speaks no English. How can he help you place an order?

One way would be to show you a menu which has photographs of the dishes on offer. The waiter might also use some gesture, perhaps pretending to drink to show you which is the drinks page of the menu. In other words, he would support your understanding using visual clues.

The principle of visual support is vital for children with speech, language and communication needs – and those learning EAL. You can use real objects (as in story sacks, for example), pictures, symbols or work that another group has already done when giving instructions, explaining a concept or reading a story. The photographs at the end of this chapter show examples of visual support.

There is developmental sequence in the type of visual support that children can cope with (Figure 7.3). The youngest children, and older children with developmental delay, will need the actual object that they know well – so if you are using the word shoe, for example, this would be the child's own shoe. At the next stage of development, it might be any shoe, not just their own. Next they might come to understand that a small toy can symbolise an object, so a doll's shoe would be appropriate. Soon they will come to understand photographs, first of objects well known to them (their own shoe), then of any shoe. Coloured pictures come next, followed by coloured then black and white pictorial symbols.

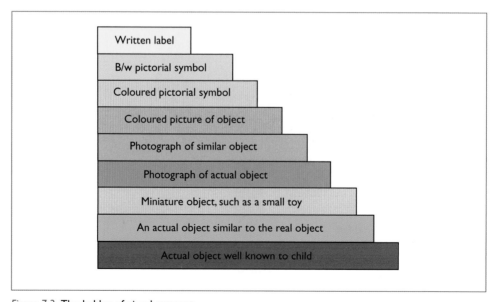

Figure 7.3 The ladder of visual support

A good example of visual support I saw was in secondary schools where subject staff provided pupils with laminated A4 placemats with pictorial symbols for key vocabulary. Figure 7.4 shows an example, from a science lesson. Figure 7.5 shows an example of visual support for exploring a behaviour incident with a student. Another great idea (Figure 7.6) was at Haverstock secondary school in London, where an agreed set of icons is used in all subject areas to indicate what types of activities pupils will engage with during a lesson – an open book for reading, a TV screen for watching film, two heads facing each other for paired work, and so on.

You may already be using visual timetables – velcro-backed pictures or symbols for literacy, maths, PE and so on, which you put up in sequence to show children what they will be doing over a morning (younger children) or a two to three day period (older children). Some children will need their own version, perhaps using photos instead of symbols, or covering shorter periods of time (up to break, perhaps, rather than the whole day).

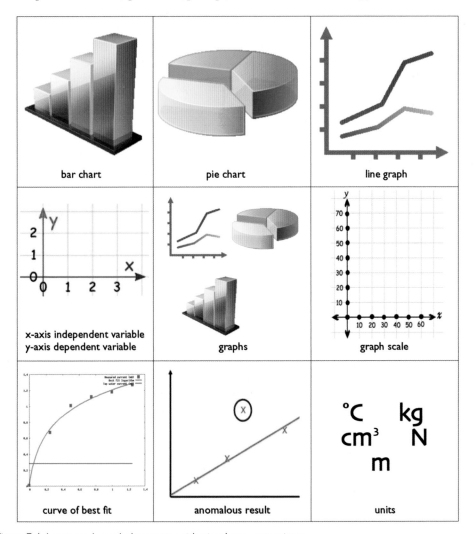

Figure 7.4 Laminated vocabulary mats with visual support: science

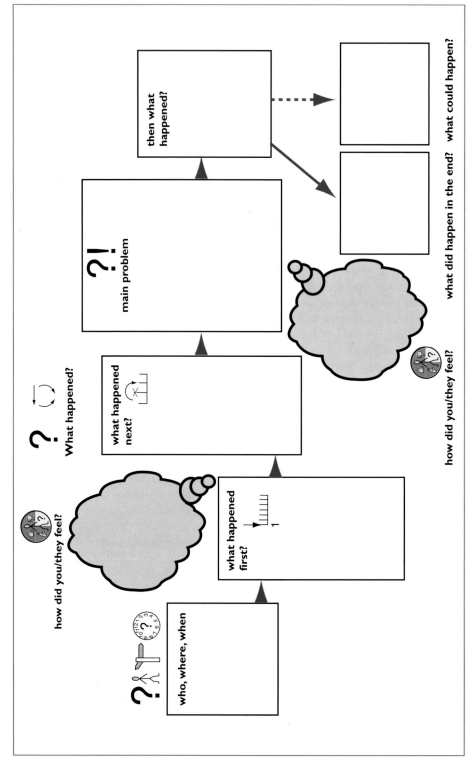

Figure 7.5 Visual support for exploring a behavioural incident with a student

In this lesson you will be learning through:

1. Watching a film clip then class discussion	
2. Writing on a questionnaire	
3. Paired work to see who has the same opinions as you	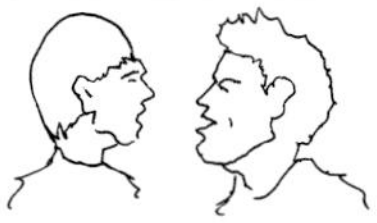
4. Small group work about your favourite conversation topics	

Figure 7.6 Icons for learning activities

Source: Haverstock school and Listen-EAR speech and language therapy project

Visual timetables show what activities are going to happen, and in what order. Also useful are task and routine boards, which remind children of what they have to do *within* an activity (a task or a routine) through a series of illustrated steps. They list jobs to be done – for example, getting ready to go home as coat, lunchbox, reading bag. An adult should go through the pictures or symbols before the activity starts, then help children manage one step then the next by referring to the board, encouraging them in time to use the board independently to guide their actions.

Graphic organisers, often used with EAL learners but beneficial for pupils with SLCN, are another form of visual support. They help children represent key relationships between ideas or objects, such as lists, cause and effect, compare/contrast. Examples are shown in Figure 7.7.

You can take stock of your setting or school's use of visual support by using a brilliant Communication Friendly Environment booklet produced as a result of collaboration between Widgit Software and Warwickshire Integrated Disability Service (www.symbolsinclusion project.org/evidence/cfe/CFE_Bookle_2008.pdf). This booklet practices what it preaches; it uses visual support (almost entirely photographs) to provide a benchmark against which schools and settings can compare themselves.

For practical ideas on how to develop your use of visual support I cannot recommend highly enough Emma Jordan and Sue Hayden's award-winning *Language for Learning* (2007) and *Language for Learning in the Secondary School* (2011) practical guides for supporting pupils with language and communication difficulties across the curriculum. There is also a Language for Learning company (www.languageforlearning.co.uk) from which you can buy these guides as well as other time-saving resources for visual support.

Retrieval charts, tables or information grids

Who?	Ate what?	When?
the hungry caterpillar	I apple	Monday
he	2 pears	Tuesday

Mini beast	Habitat	Food	Predators
beetle			

Flow diagram

```
┌──────┐      ┌──────┐      ┌──────┐
│      │ ───→ │      │ ───→ │      │
└──────┘      └──────┘      └──────┘
```

For example, how we get our milk.

Timeline

└──┴───┴───┴───┴───┴───┴───┴───┴───┘

Cycle

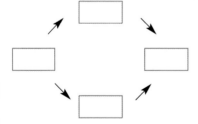

For example, life cycles, daily routines, and so on.

Figure 7.7 Examples of graphic organisers

Cause – effect

For example, 'Erosion is caused by rainfall', 'A decline in the manufacturing industry led to high unemployment.', 'Because of this the queen became more and more despondent'.

Cause	Effect 1
	Effect 1

Problem – solution

Scaffold as for cause and effect.

Compare – contrast

Life in a village in Pakistan	Life in a city in Pakistan
Lanterns used to light the way at night	Street lights
Narrow streets	Wide roads
Clay ovens in the courtyard	Modern gas cookers
People go to bed early	People are out and about in the evening
Water comes from a pump	Water comes from a tap

Ways in which they are the same	Ways in which they are different

Biographies		
Nelson Mandela	**Both**	**Ghandi**

Venn diagrams would be an appropriate alternative visual here.

Figure 7.7 continued

Main idea with further details

These can be differentiated for pupils with different needs in a variety of ways, for example by providing headings and sub-headings.

Key visuals include the following.

Pyramids *(hierarchy of ideas)*

Tree diagrams

Structured overviews

Figure 7.7 continued

Finally, there are a couple of great websites I came across which provide children with direct access to visually supported material. ITV's Signed Stories (www.signedstories.com) has a huge range of animated versions of the best children's picture books, signed in British Sign Language. The Children's Society's Askability website (www.askability.org.uk) provides young people with symbol-supported access to a range of information – news, sport, 'what's on', soaps, blogs and so on.

What if the child doesn't seem to understand?

'The single biggest problem in communication is the illusion it has taken place', said George Bernard Shaw, and nowhere is this more evident than children with SLCN, who may give every appearance of understanding and yet be lost in the classroom, unable to make sense of the language that surrounds them.

These children may be one step behind the others because they are watching to copy what they do. They may in reading learn to decode well but seem to struggle to answer simple questions about what they have read. They may smile sweetly, and be no trouble to anyone, or they may misbehave.

To help us understand their needs, it is useful to return to the holiday example and now imagine you have been on holiday for a month or so and can understand some of the language. How do you need people to communicate with you? You'll probably want them to speak slowly, in short, simple sentences, and with pauses so you can catch up.

Again, the same principles apply to children with SLCN. It's important to keep instructions short – much everyday classroom language ('When you come in from washing your hands you should sit at the front not the back because if you sit at the back all the others will have to climb over you to find somewhere to sit') is too long for most children, never mind those with SLCN. The child with language comprehension difficulties may only pick up and act on the last few words (here, 'find somewhere to sit'). This can often get them into trouble. So it is helpful to 'chunk' teacher talk, breaking long sentences down into several shorter ones (Table 7.3) and where possible avoiding embedded clauses – 'You can find the diagrams at the end of the chapter' rather than 'The page the diagrams are on is at the end of the chapter.'

'Before', and 'after' can cause problems too. Try to give instructions in the order in which they are to be carried out, using 'first' and 'next' or 'then': 'First, put the title and date at the top. Then draw your diagram', rather than 'Before you draw your diagram remember to put the title and date at the top'.

Table 7.3 Breaking sentences down

Instead of ...	Say ...
If one person in your group is lighting the candle I want the other person to put the beaker down over the candle and then we're going to use our wonderful observation skills to see what happens.	I want one person to light the candle. Then the other person will put the beaker upside down over the candle. Watch to see what happens. So what are we going to do?

For some children with SLCN, idiom and metaphor causes problems – phrases that don't mean what they say, like 'Pull your socks up', 'It goes in one ear and out the other', 'She'll go up the wall', 'Don't bite off more than you can chew', 'That was spot on.' It is amazing how much of classroom talk involves such non-literal language. Research (Lazar *et al.*, 1989) has shown that one in five of teachers' instructions contain at least one idiom. So it's not easy to avoid them, but it is possible to become more conscious of when they are used. One teacher I know enlists the help of the class in telling her when she has used non-literal language, so she can explain it. Others teach an idiom of the week, having pupils illustrate the literal then the actual meaning of phrases like 'I'm all ears', 'He's in hot water'. The box below has some ideas for idioms that children can have fun illustrating.

Idioms to illustrate

A blanket ban on mobile phones
Sorry, I'm tied up right now
It goes in one ear and out the other
It's raining cats and dogs
You're pulling my leg
Get off your high horse
You're in hot water
You're driving me up the wall
Her stomach was tied up in knots

If a child has any sort of comprehension difficulty, a key strategy is to encourage them to always let others know that they have not understood, and ask for clarification. In Chapter 6 we looked at ways of teaching this strategy to a whole class; for children with SLCN this teaching may need to be reinforced by further repetition and practice with a teaching assistant or support teacher. The adult can set up specific situations to allow the child to practise seeking clarification – giving extra-long instructions, for example, speaking too quickly or using words that are not in the child's vocabulary. The child can also be provided with their own personalised key ring of cards to use to ask the other person to speak more slowly, explain a word meaning and so on. The teacher will need to check for comprehension by asking the child to explain what they have to do in their own words.

What if I can't understand a child's speech or they use incorrect language?

One group of children who often worry practitioners and teachers most is those with speech difficulties, who have lots to say but aren't easily intelligible to others.

The ability to articulate sounds is still developing in children under seven years of age. It's normal for a three-year-old not to be able to say sounds like 'sh', 'ch', 'th' and 'r'. Many four-year-olds won't yet have mastered 'r' (as in rabbit), 'l' (as in letter) 'th' (as in thumb), 'sh' (as in show), and 'j' (as in jam). Not until they are seven can children reliably use 'r', 'th', and clusters of consonants like 'sp', 'fr', 'scr' and so on.

You can help by making sure the child has plenty of opportunities to hear correct pronunciation. Try repeating back what they have said, in a natural way, in the correct form – if the child says 'I like his punny pace', try 'I like his funny face too. What a funny face! Do you know what that man with the funny face is called?' This way the child gets several chances to hear 'funny face' modelled.

Some children with articulation problems are helped by a 'communication book', with a selection of pictures or photos or symbols to point to in order to get their meaning across. If you are not sure what they mean, it's best not to pretend you have understood. Instead, ask them to try again using different words, mime or pictures. You can say 'I'm sorry I didn't manage to understand – we can try again later'. Using a home-school book, in which parents write about things that happened at home, may make it easier to understand what the child is trying so hard to tell you.

If the child stammers it is especially important to stay relaxed. Try slowing down your own rate of talking, and avoid completing the child's sentences for them. Give them plenty of opportunities to communicate in situations where they are most likely to be fluent – talking about a special interest, singing, reciting rhymes. Comment sympathetically on the emotions or events that may be causing a bout of stammering ('I can see you're really cross', 'Oooh, that knee must hurt'), but not on the stammer itself. And never, ever ask them to start again at the beginning of the sentence – that is the most likely place for the stammering to occur.

What if they can't answer questions in class?

One of the most powerful forms of professional development for teachers I saw was training by speech and language therapists in how to match questioning to different children's stages of thinking. The training was based on the work of Marion Blank, who described four levels of questions, moving from concrete to abstract. These levels are described and illustrated in Table 7.4.

Appropriate support for children's language and thinking will involve identifying roughly where in this sequence of levels a child is, asking questions at that level but also seeking to move them on to the next level by modelling and scaffolding.

Planning for differentiation

One of the more depressing moments in my time as Communication Champion was when we were preparing materials for 'No Pens Day Wednesday'. To do this we looked at and tried to adapt a pile of everyday lesson plans in primary and secondary schools. Most of the plans had a column for or note on differentiation. Sadly, it seemed from these plans that the only differentiation strategy known to the teachers involved was to have a teaching assistant work with the 'lower-ability' children. Yet we know from important research at the Institute of Education (Blatchford et al., 2012) that this approach is unlikely to enable children with additional needs to make progress. Indeed, the research has shown that it may have the opposite effect, actually reducing children's rate of progress when compared with children with similar characteristics receiving less teaching assistant support.

Far better are differentiation strategies that enable children with SEN to work independently, through the use of 'access strategies' or 'reasonable adjustments' – strategies which find a way round the barriers to learning that the child experiences.

Table 7.4 Differentiating questions

Level 1

Level 1 questions relate to the immediate environment and require concrete thinking. Children are asked to match, identify and name objects. Most two- to three-year-olds can cope with questions like these.	Examples: Find one like this. What's this? Who is this? What colour is this? What did the ... say? What is X doing? What can you see? Show me the ...

Level 2

At Level 2, the level of the average three- to four-year-old, children are able to move beyond simple identification; their thinking involves some analysis such as classifying/ grouping objects, describing things and understanding object functions.	Examples: What is happening? What is this for? What does it do? Tell me about this thing? What things did we see? Who is ...? Where was ...? When did ...? What did he do? How are these different? What else is a X? (category, such as a fruit) Show me something that is a (category).

Level 3

Level 3 questions ask the child to use their own knowledge to make basic predictions, assume the role of another, describe a sequence of events or make generalisations. Most four- to five-year-olds can think at this level.	Examples: What will happen next? What is ... going to say? How do you think he feels? How did he ...? How else could he do it? What have they done so far? How are these same? How do I make ... (e.g. a sandwich)? What is a ...? (definitions) What happened to all these... (e.g. when I put them in water)? Give me another example ...

Level 4

At Level 4, typical of children of five and above, children's thinking goes well beyond the concrete; they use language to solve problems, make predictions, suggest solutions and give explanations.	Examples: What will happen if ...? How can we tell? How did you know? Why did you choose that one? How did that happen? What could he do? What would you do if...? Why is it made of that? Why can't we ... (e.g. eat ice cream with a knife and fork?) If you were X, what would you say/do?

Table 7.5 lists such strategies for children who need extra support with understanding or using language. Highlighting just one or two key strategies from the strategy bank for each child, each term, can be a useful approach. Most of these strategies are equally applicable to EAL learners; Table 7.6 sets out some of the similarities and differences between strategies appropriate to children with SEN in language and communication, and those learning a second language. Putting this into practice, Tables 7.7, 7.8 and 7.9 illustrate lesson plans that make use of appropriate differentiation.

Interestingly, research is beginning to show that where teachers adopt appropriate differentiation following training in strategies to support pupils with SLCN, this alone can have a direct impact on these pupils' language abilities and attainment. Speech and language therapist Julia Starling (2011) provided mainstream secondary teachers in Australia with training on classroom strategies as shown below:

- Direct vocabulary instruction
    - Identification of key vocabulary for new topics ('10 Key Words')
    - Interactive creation of relevant descriptors/ definitions
- Information processing
    - Breaking down texts: mapping central idea, associated facts/details
    - Supplementing verbal/print information with visuals
- Teachers' written language
    - Modifying the language of worksheets, assignments and tests
    - Changing the sequence of presented information e.g. text and questions layout
- Teachers' oral language
    - Slower speech rate, or better voice projection
    - Facing the class, not the board
    - Repetition of key facts

A similar 'control group' school was identified which was awaiting the training. 22 students with specific language impairments in the 'experimental' and 22 in the 'control' school were identified, aged 12–14 years. The students were given tests of written expression and listening comprehension before and after the teacher training period, and then one and two terms later. Results showed a positive impact on both measures, which was sustained over time without further direct support.

Additional interventions

So far in this chapter we have looked at basic strategies which every teacher needs to have in their toolkit in order to provide inclusive 'Wave 1' quality first teaching for pupils needing support with language and communication. Support for these pupils may also, however, require additional interventions, over and above effective everyday classroom practice.

What form should these interventions take? When children have been identified as having speech, language and communication needs it is all too easy to believe that the only response should be referral to a speech and language therapist, who will whisk them away, treat them and send them back to the setting or classroom 'fixed'.

My time as Communication Champion gave me much evidence that this approach is unlikely to be successful, for two reasons. First, there are not and never will be enough speech and language therapists to treat all the children (well over 50 per cent in areas of social deprivation, remember) who need additional intervention. Second, because even if there were, language-learning opportunities happen round the clock and language is learned best in natural contexts. So the most effective practice will involve specialists like speech and language therapists in advising and supporting those who are in day to day contact with the child, so that they know what to do to maximise the child's learning.

Some children – those with the greatest difficulties – may need direct therapy, backed up by this 'round-the-clock' support from the adults who spend most time with them. Others, however, may not need to see a therapist at all, but can catch up with their peers as a result of planned intervention undertaken by school and setting staff who have had the necessary training and support from specialists.

The following case studies provide some examples.

CASE STUDY: EARLY YEARS

Gunter primary school in Birmingham took part in the Every Child a Talker initiative. When Alex joined the nursery at the age of three, she was well below what would be expected of a child her age in all aspects of development, but particularly in communication and language. She used one or two words, but otherwise communicated non-verbally, using actions and banging objects to gain attention, and screaming if frustrated.

The Every Child a Talker monitoring tool enabled her key worker to establish exactly where she was in each aspect of language. Listening and attention and social skills (using language in 'conversations') emerged as the areas with the greatest delay. The key worker then sought expert advice from the Every Child a Talker consultant and put into place a plan of action.

All staff were asked to spend some one to one time with Alex during the day, playing alongside her and providing a running commentary on her actions. All non-verbal attempts at communication were acknowledged and praised, with staff sensitively interpreting and responding to her meaning. If she spoke, they would expand her utterance by repeating it back with one word added. The key worker kept a book of Alex's vocabulary, which all staff looked at and added to. The training which staff had experienced helped them to understand that she would need to hear new words repeated many, many times in different situations before she was able to use them, and the importance of building up from one to two word utterances, then later from two to three words.

As a result of this planned intervention, Alex made more than two years progress in listening and attention, 18 months progress in understanding language and around six months progress in her talk. This is now the area being targeted, with plans to involve Alex's parents by sharing key messages about repeated use of vocabulary, commenting on Alex's play and expanding her speech. Her parents will also take part in specific training, such as dialogic book talk, which Every Child a Talker has to offer.

Table 7.5 Strategy sheet: speech, language and communication difficulty

Giving instructions/ teacher talk	Use pupil's name before asking a question or giving an instruction.
	Give directions before an activity, not during it.
	Keep verbal instructions simple, and in the order you want them carried out. Be aware of how many 'information-carrying' words you are using: 'Get your **maths book** from the pile on **my desk**; on a **clean page**, **write** the **date** and then **copy down** the **calculations on the board'** has more information-carrying words than many adults will be able to remember.
	Check for understanding – ask the pupil to tell you what they have to do.
	Agree a private signal pupil can use to show you they have not understood, or teach them to say 'Sorry, I didn't understand that – can you say it again, please?' Praise them for asking for clarification.
	Support your oral presentations/explanations with pictures, real objects or mime. Use visuals (real objects, photographs, symbols) appropriate to pupil's developmental level rather than chronological age.
	Use symbols to support spoken language and text (www.widgit.com).
	Cue pupil in to a change of topic of conversation/presentation – say 'Now we are going to talk about …'.
	Pair pupil with a study buddy to repeat instructions and demonstrate tasks.
	Explain idioms, jokes, ambiguous language.
Asking questions	Give pupil time (at least 10 seconds) to respond and then, if necessary, repeat what you said. Use the same words unless you think the vocabulary was too difficult to understand
	Question pupil after some other pupils have given examples of what is required
	Give pupil time to think, or to talk to a partner before answering a question, or say 'I'm going to come back to you in a minute to ask you XXX. But first I'm going to ask Y a question.'
	If pupil can't answer a question, scaffold/support till they can rather than saying 'Can anyone help X?'
	Use a hierarchy of questions – start with an open question ('What do you think might happen next?'), then if support is needed frame the question as alternatives ('Do you think X or Y?')
	Use question prompt card to help pupils know how to respond (e.g. 'Where?' question requires a place).
Vocabulary	When you start a new topic, develop a class chart of the vocabulary that pupils will find useful or need to learn. Teach each word by helping children build a web of associations – what it sounds like, what it means, how it fits in a sentence, what words go with it.
	Put up a list of key vocabulary for a particular topic or lesson and review/re-teach the meaning of each word.
	If you can, arrange for parents or a support assistant to pre-teach key vocabulary before pupils meet it in the lesson.

Table 7.5 continued

Supporting pupil's talk and writing	Accept pupil's spoken utterances but rephrase and give them back in a grammatically correct and expanded version.
	Support oral work with talk frames /key phrases ('First … next … finally', 'I think … but on the other hand').
	Talk aloud about what you are doing using statements which give children examples of the language they might use.
	Provide topic-related role-play opportunities and model the language to be used in role-play.
	Support writing with writing frames and lists of vocabulary to choose from
	Use a range of ways of recording so that learning is not limited by the pupil's ability to write full English sentences: ● bullet points and mind maps; ● ordering tasks – for example, ordering cut-out words to make a sentence, or sentences to make a sequence of instructions; ● matching tasks, such as matching labels to pictures/diagrams/maps; ● cloze procedure, where they fill in missing words in text; ● annotating a print-off of IWB page; ● PowerPoint presentations; ● making posters, oral presentations, dramatic reconstructions.
Learning	Use teaching assistant for pre-tutoring – preparing pupil for a task so that they come to it already knowing the key vocabulary and concepts.
	Begin work on a new topic with pupil's existing knowledge and experiences – make a mind map or other visual representation of what they already know.
	Use cued listening – give pupil a small number of questions that they will have to answer after listening to teacher presentation or video input.
	Use visual timetables to show what will happen over a period of time, a visual plan of what will happen during a lesson and refer to it as the lesson progresses ('this is where we are now'), or visual task boards to show step-by-step instructions for activities or routines.
	Display classroom rules and routines, illustrated by pictures, for pupil to refer to. Illustrate them visually – for example, use a traffic light system to indicate whether pupils can talk, symbols for different noise levels (partner voices, group voices, classroom voice, playground voices), photographs of the behaviour expected in specific situations.
	Use visual summaries of discussions – mind maps, flow charts, diagrams, comic strip format, graphic organisers (www.graphic.org).
	Provide the pupil with a study pack – glossaries of key subject vocabulary, highlighter pens, glue stick, post-it notes, index cards to make their own mind maps/cartoon strips/key word lists, templates for writing up science experiments etc.
	Allow extra time to complete tasks and be aware of the fatigue the pupil may experience because of the amount of effort they have to put in to learning.
	Write down homework for pupil, or give it on a pre-printed sticky label or sheet they can stick into their book, or record your instructions on a dictaphone. Allocate a homework buddy they can ring if they have forgotten what to do ('phone a friend').

Table 7.6 Learning and teaching for EAL learners and those with SEN (SLCN)

Strategies for EAL learners	Strategies for both EAL learners and those with SEN (SLCN)	Strategies for those with SEN (SLCN)
Respect for learners' first language and culture – e.g. use of first language in the classroom, inviting parents in to provide input		
Role models of successful adults from minority ethnic groups		Role models of successful disabled adults
Work with families to value cultural heritage	Consistency between home and school, valuing the partnership with parents/carers	Work with parents to help them develop the child's language, use symbols, use home-school diary to support child's communication, etc.
Rich visual environment with many supports	Visual supports – e.g. pictures to accompany speech	For some children, uncluttered visual environment to reduce distractions and help child to focus
Pairing child to work with another child who shares their first language	Pairing child with a study buddy – e.g. for paired reading of a text	
	Use of symbols to support spoken language and text (www.widgit.com)	
	Gesture and signing – BSL, Makaton, etc.	Signing training for all staff
	Explicit teaching of language structures and features (e.g. time connectives, verbs)	Explicit teaching of pragmatics – how to be a good speaker and listener
	Explicit practice of language structures in meaningful contexts – e.g. having done task, now instruct another group in how to do it, or use of barrier games	
	Repeated use of a language structure so children get familiar with it (e.g. 'Your story is finished')	Work on very early language concepts (e.g. clean/dirty)
	Support for remembering heard language patterns (e.g. hearing something again on a tape)	For some children, slower pace and more repetition when learning new concepts
		Overlearning – increased opportunities to practise a skill until it becomes automatic

Table 7.6 continued

Strategies for EAL learners	Strategies for both EAL learners and those with SEN (SLCN)	Strategies for those with SEN (SLCN)
Use of first language/ translation dictionaries, dual language materials	Use of glossaries and dictionaries	
	Scaffolding new language structure/ideas by practising first with familiar contexts	
	Key words on the wall, with pictures	
	Flexible groupings: • use of paired talk to give children confidence • groupings that provide good language role models when children are working independently • groupings of children at same language level for direct teaching	
	Adults not interrupting	
	If child uses incorrect speech the adult does not correct it, but models back a correct and full sentence or an expanded one	
	Giving children processing time after asking a question or giving an instruction	
	Multi-sensory approaches and practical activities	
	Start with the concrete – build from this into more abstract language	
	Use of story props, real objects, artefacts	
	Begin work on a new topic with child's existing knowledge and experiences – make a mind map or other visual representation of what they already know	
	Targeted and differentiated questioning	
	Teacher and teaching assistant model the task and the language before the children work independently	

Table 7.6 continued

Strategies for EAL learners	Strategies for both EAL learners and those with SEN (SLCN)	Strategies for those with SEN (SLCN)
	Teacher shortens sentences and simplifies vocabulary when giving instructions; asks a child to repeat instructions	Teacher gears the language structures s/he uses to whether child understands sentences with one, two, three or more information-carrying words
	Prompt cards, with pictures, to remind children what to do	
	Children have opportunity to see other children model a task (e.g. by feeding back in plenary) before they undertake it themselves	
	Opportunities for children to re-tell a story with props	
	If child can't answer a question, teacher scaffolds/supports till they can rather than saying 'Can anyone help X?'	
	Visual timetables	
	Use of assessment data to pinpoint precise learning needs	
	Use of mini whiteboards to make it safe to respond in whole-class teaching	
	Ask children to underline words they don't understand and look up their meaning in a dictionary	
	Identify new and difficult words and explain their meaning	
	Provide sentence starters, writing frames, key visuals	
	Forced alternatives – provide child with a choice of two sentences/ideas and they say their choice	
	Joint planning and lesson delivery with EAL or speech and language specialists	
	Consistency in sign, gesture, symbols used by all the adults in the class	
	Use of drama and role play	

Table 7.7 Differentiation in lesson plans – Year 3

Class:	Teacher:	Date:	Lesson: English – Traditional Tales
Learning objective: • To listen to a traditional tale and identify the common features • To use descriptive vocabulary to describe characters		**Previous learning:** To listen to and discuss a traditional tale and then analyse the structure	**Speaking and listening objective:** Use intonation to make speech more interesting for listeners

Activity	Differentiation	Resource
Starter: **Quiz** What do children remember about traditional tales? What are the key features? How many traditional tales do they remember? Ask the children specific questions, such as: • Tell me one of the key features of a traditional tale • What is your favourite traditional tale that we have done so far? • Who is your favourite/worst hero/villain? • Recap on the key vocabulary words for traditional tales	Mixed ability pairs/groups Cut-out characters on a stick for 'hero', 'heroine', 'villain', to hold up while telling Rumpelstiltskin story and giving instructions on task Visuals (picture cards) for the main parts of the story (e.g. setting, problem, resolution)	
Vocabulary: Traditional, tale, hero, heroine, villain, character, intonation Teach vocabulary using what it means like/what it sounds like/what it means/words that go with it/put it in a sentence		
Main: • Read Rumpelstiltskin. Identify as a group the hero, heroine and villain and the main parts of the story. • Children to work in pairs. Each pair to decide on three descriptive words for each character. • Children make groups of four. Share their ideas; identify three new descriptive words for each character. • Groups merge to form groups of eight. Children discuss the list of descriptive words they have identified so far, and generate as many more as they can for each character. If necessary, model and guide them to think of personality traits as well as more obvious physical characteristics. • Each group to nominate a representative to play each character. • As a class, brainstorm the descriptive words for the hero. The children playing that character act in a way that represents that descriptive word e.g. brave, mean. Take a photo of the child acting. • Repeat this activity for the heroine and villain. • Photos of each child can be used to make a poster for each character.	Teaching assistant to pre-teach some descriptive words to some children Provide forced alternatives if necessary – is he kind or mean? And extend from there. Think of another word that is the same as 'kind'	The book Rumpelstiltskin

Plenary:

- Choose several children to take the parts of the different characters. Children to retell the story, making sure they act the descriptive words that have been identified for each character.
- What effect does this have on the listener? Is the listener more or less interested because of this?
- All children to have a go at speaking a particular passage with and without intonation so they can experience and identify the difference.

Assessment for learning: The rest of the class are to peer assess – are they using intonation in their speech? Children to identify where they're using intonation? Which words are being stressed? What difference does it make?

Homework: Each child to go home and tell an adult three descriptive words for the hero, heroine and villain

Table 7.8 Differentiation in lesson plans – Year 5

Class:	Teacher:	Date:	Science: Moving and Growing – The Heart

Learning objective:
To investigate the workings of the heart by comparing with the actions of a pump.

(Based on lesson freely available from Science Museum of Minnesota at http://www.smm.org/heart/lessons/lesson5a.htm)

Previous learning:
- Functions and locations of major organs in the body
- Location and function of the heart

Speaking and listening objectives:
3a: Make contributions relevant to the topic and take turns in discussion
3b: Vary contributions to suit the activity and purpose, including exploratory and tentative comments where ideas are being collected together, and reasoned, evaluative comments as discussion moves to conclusions or actions

Activity	Differentiation	Resource

Activity

Starter:
Round robin – pupils say what they already know about the heart

Vocabulary: Pump, valve, vein, artery, flow, stethoscope
Recap key vocabulary – valve, vein and artery. Use a visual organiser to contrast the functions of each. Teach vocabulary using what it sounds like/what it means/words that go with it/put it in a sentence.

Main activity:
- Talking partners: Where in your body is your heart?
  1. Using virtual stethoscope at http://www.smm.org/heart/heart/steth.htm – ask pupils to describe where in the body they think the heart is. E.g. – below shoulder, left side, right side, under collar bone, in middle of chest. Check their ideas with the virtual stethoscope
  2. Use animation at http://www.smm.org/heart/heart/pumping.htm to show how the heart pumps, and the valves open and close.
- Tell the pupils they are going to make their own pump.
- In mixed ability groups, pupils have a set of resources and written instructions of how to make the heart pump.
- Pupils read and follow instructions to build the model.

Differentiation

Teaching assistant to pre-teach vocabulary to some pupils

Picture prompts for lower-achieving – e.g. diagram of heart

Make an audio recording of the instructions for making the pump, or pair good with weaker readers

Chunk or simplify information for similarities and differences discussion.
For example:
- Name one thing that is the same
- Name one thing that is different

Resource

Lesson plan and animations available at www.smm.org/heart/lessons/lesson5a.htm

For each group -
- wide mouth jar (plastic)
- balloons
- skewer
- two flexible straws
- scissors
- bowl to collect water spills
- sponge
- a set of the written instructions for the activity

Video camera to film activity

• Once model is complete pupils to discuss in groups:
  – What are the similarities and differences between the heart and the pump you assembled? (key question)
  – Remove the balloon flap (valve) from the apparatus. What happened?
  – Does the valve affect how well the water flows?
  – What happens when the valve is removed?
  – Extension: can you think of other examples of valves and pumps?		

Plenary: • Recap learning: Share answers to questions; teacher targeted questioning to target understanding of all within the group. Paired talk: What might happen to a person if the valves in their heart did not work or wore out? How can we look after out heart? What can be done to repair damage? • In groups pupils list five key points on how to keep a healthy heart.		
Assessment for learning: How would you summarise the workings of the heart – indicate with traffic lights how confident you are in your summary. How well do you think you took turns in the discussion?		**Homework:** Measure your pulse beat at different times of the day. When is it fastest? And slowest? What is your Dad's/Mum's pulse rate?

Table 7.9 Differentiation in lesson plans – Year 7

Year/Class: 7	Teacher:	Date:	Scheme of work: Fibres and Fabrics Lesson topic: Fibres and Fabric Constructions

Learning objectives:
- To give examples of natural and man-made fibres and to identify where they come from
- To identify the main characteristics of some of the fibres
- To identify two different constructions of fabric

Speaking and listening objective:
Talk using sentences of around 7–11 words

Key questions/concepts:
- What do we mean by textiles?
- Why are textiles important to society?
- What do we mean by natural fibres
- What do we mean by man-made fibres?
- What are the characteristics of this fibre?
- Where do natural/ man-made fibres come from?
- How are fibres made into fabrics?

Resources:
- Photos of a range of familiar textiles made from a variety of fibres (complete/partial images)
- The Fabric of Society by Mrs Zubairy, Edenham High (www.youtube.com/watch?v=eCqsEaYv70s)
- Range of fabric samples made from a variety of fibres
- A favourite item of clothing each student has been asked to bring from home
- Flashcard-sized cards: name of fibre, description of where it comes from and/or main characteristics
- A/B/C/D cards for multiple choices
- Keywords display

Starter: Guess what? Work in pairs
- Identify what the item is from a photo that shows only a part of it (e.g. towel, leotard, swimming shorts, sports fleece, sock, gloves, rucksack, jumper, scarf, cap, curtains, table cloth, pillow, flag, teddy bear, etc.). Sort into three piles whether the item is made from 'man-made fibres', 'natural fibres' or 'either'.
- Show complete photo of items (on slides). Discuss which category each belongs to.

Vocabulary: Textiles, natural, man-made/synthetic, chemicals, fibres/yarn, fabric/fabric construction, woven/knitted, characteristics/properties
Teach vocabulary using what it sounds like/what it means/words that go with it /put it in a sentence

Main:
Introduce 'textiles'
Find a common link between all the photos shown – the word 'textiles' refers to any item made out of fabric. Highlight and refer to keywords display.

YouTube presentation: The Fabric of Society
Reinforce information using 'Who Wants To Be A Millionaire' format quiz.
Questions to highlight information relating to:

- Why are textiles important to society?
- What are natural fibres/man-made fibres?
- What are the characteristics of this fibre?
- Where do natural/man-made fibres come from?
- How are fibres made into fabrics?

Students work in groups of five. Each question to be answered by a different student – hold up either A/B/C/D card. If unsure, can ask team members, 'phone a friend', 'ask the audience' or request answers card for 50:50. Students hold up answer card when asked 'What's your final answer?'

What is it made out of?

Work in pairs to decide what fabrics/fibres the favourite items of clothing brought from home are made of, and the features of the fabric (e.g. 'This is made of natural fibres so it doesn't make me feel hot when I'm dancing'), **or** match name of fibre to description of where it comes from/characteristics and to each fabric sample supplied by teacher (linen, cotton, nylon, wool, silk, viscose, Lycra, acrylic, polyester)

Whole class feedback to include whether the fabric is knitted or woven.

Going shopping! In pairs

You are planning to buy a new item of clothing – jumper/coat/trousers etc. Explain to your partner what fabric would you want it made of and why – justify why you want that fabric

Plenary/assessment for learning:
Guess which one? (Whole class)

- Teacher describes a specific fibre, students to identify what the fabric sample is – e.g. 'This is *man-made. It's very strong and light weight. Kites and tents are made out of this'* (nylon)
- Each pair gives a description of a fabric for others to guess
- Peer assessment on the speaking and listening objective – how well did people do in using longer sentences for their descriptions of fabrics?
- Say which activity in the lesson you found most useful and why

Differentiation strategies:

- Demonstrate and model examples of description and justification
- Picture/icon for each of keywords. Display, explain and refer to these. For some students put on laminated word mats on tables.
- Whole class 'think time' before answering the questions asked
- Differentiated questions in quiz, using Bloom's taxonomy for questions: Can you name the...? Can you tell why...? Find the meaning of...? What is...? Which is true or false...? Can you explain in your own words...? Can you distinguish between...? What differences exist between...? Can you provide a definition for...?
- Provide some students with a talk frame for 'Going shopping' activity: 'I would buy...because...'
- Some students select from a choice of three fabrics (plenary activity)

CASE STUDY: DAISY

Daisy, aged three and a half, attended a pre-school setting in Cornwall, also involved in Every Child a Talker. She was picked up by the setting as delayed in her expressive language and social skills. She also had difficulties with some speech sounds. She was referred to the speech and language therapy service and a student speech and language therapist went into the setting to run Phase 1 activities from the 'Letters and Sounds' programme, which help children discriminate sounds. The Every Child a Talker speech and language therapist consultant provided training to staff on the 'Learning Language and Loving It' Hanen programme.

Observation by the Every Child a Talker teacher consultant showed that Daisy lacked confidence and often did not engage with activities or other children. With the help of the consultant, staff planned ways of building her confidence and participation. They gave her a special job (watering the plants), built on her interests by engaging her in dressing up and doll play, and provided role-play activities where she could talk on a toy phone rather than have to talk directly to others. Strong links were formed with Daisy's mother, who was encouraged to come into the setting regularly and share in planning the next steps – like developing Daisy's use of prepositions by modelling them in doll play ('...*in* the bath', '...*next to* the bath', 'standing *behind* the buggy'). Finding that Daisy communicated more in smaller, more intimate spaces, staff created cosy corners – for example using hanging drapes inside and a tent outside with bay leaves and other herbs in it.

As a result of what the Every Child a Talker consultants call 'small things, done consistently over a period of time', Daisy soon caught up. She no longer shows delay on any aspect of the Every Child a Talker child monitoring tool.

CASE STUDY: PRIMARY

At Foley Park primary in Worcestershire, which we met briefly in Chapter 3, high numbers of children experience language and communication difficulties. 'We noticed about three years ago that pupils were increasingly arriving at school with little vocabulary, even for words you would expect them to know such as "cow" or "horse"', says the head teacher. Children were referred for speech and language therapy, but therapists were only able to see around twenty of the school's pupils a year, which did not begin to meet the identified needs.

The speech and language therapy service suggested that they work with the school in a different way. They trained staff to run a small group narrative intervention programme, and introduced Language Link screening and intervention in Reception. All staff were trained in how to teach vocabulary and listening skills, and how to use visual support for language. Photographs, signs and symbols are regularly used throughout the school, with visual timetables, task and routine boards in every classroom. A team of three highly trained teaching assistants work with individual children with SLCN, providing one-to-one or small group support.

The impact of this work has been significant. Behaviour is good across the whole school, which staff attribute to the visual support systems. On entry to the Reception class in 2010/11 nearly 60 per cent of the class were identified as having difficulties. By the end of the year, 87 per cent of the class scored within age-related expectations on Language Link assessments, and no child was at the level indicating need for referral to a speech and language therapist

CASE STUDY: SECONDARY

Beal High School in Redbridge, which we met earlier in this chapter, has a resourced provision for social and communication difficulties, and over 80 pupils with statements across the provision and the main school. 25 per cent of pupils on the SEN register have SLCN as their main need, and another 14 per cent have autism spectrum disorders (ASD) – so work on speech, language and communication has a high profile.

The school worked with a nearby university speech and language therapy department on a programme called Enhancing Language and Communication in Secondary Schools (ELCISS). All staff had training on SLCN and how it presents in the classroom. This was followed by focused work by departments with the local authority specialist teaching team, and speech and language therapist input.

The science department chose to focus on vocabulary. Teachers and departmental teaching assistants explored ways of presenting key words at the start of each lesson, accompanied by visuals. Special multisensory equipment was bought, such as a large model of a plant cell with labels to attach, for teaching assistants to use with groups.

Staff also learned to modify their own language, using less irony and sarcasm, reducing the amount of teacher talk, getting children to come up with their own questions, chunking instructions and giving them in the order in which they are to be carried out.

A recently qualified speech and language therapist was then engaged to work in the school three days a week, supported by a more experienced therapist from the local team. Together they work with speech and language champions in each department, on schemes of work, lesson plans and assessment. The school-based therapist had same type of induction as the school's newly qualified teachers, developing a blend of skills that will be a great resource to the local speech and language therapy service, and to other schools in future.

Support for students with identified needs is provided at Wave 2 through small-group narrative and vocabulary intervention programmes. The City University team trained Higher Level Teaching assistants (HLTAs) to run these twelve-week programmes for Year 7/8 students. Subsequent tracking showed the impact; the 18 students involved made an average two levels of progress in English over Key Stage 3, having left primary school at levels P8 to 4C. Small group social skills interventions are also provided in Key Stage 3, where required.

At Wave 3, students with more severe needs is provided through a speech, language and communication support plan developed by a speech and language therapist or a specialist from the local authority outreach service. An HLTA who has had all the ELCISS training meets the specialist and they plan together who will do what to support the pupil – for example the outreach teacher might include the pupil in a group working on questioning or vocabulary, while the HLTA might provide input to the pupil on social skills.

Most support is provided in Year 7, with reducing amounts in Years 8 and 9. By the end of Key Stage 3 only a tiny number of students still need intervention at Wave 3. This is a clear indicator of the success of the model of partnership with specialists developed at Beal.

What works at Wave 2?

Some intervention at Wave 2, particularly in the early years, can take the form of carefully planned strategies for increasing and improving the child's daily interactions with adults over the course of ordinary activities at home and in the setting, as we have seen.

Other types of Wave 2 interventions, particularly for school-age children, take the form of additional small group sessions delivered over a period of one or two terms, usually by trained teaching assistants. It is important that schools make sure that their provision map has these school-based Wave 2 interventions in place for children with language delay. Speech and language therapists' skills can be used to train and support school-based staff in providing these interventions, so as to maximise the time they have available for children with more severe and specific language impairments.

Wave 2 language interventions are proliferating across the country. Table 7.10 shows some of the most widely used interventions for speech and language difficulties; Table 7.11 covers interventions for children with social communication difficulties/autism. In both tables, interventions which have been shown to have impact through published evaluation using any sort of 'pre-' and 'post-' intervention measures are asterisked.

This does not mean that the other interventions are not effective – just that it will be important to check at school level that you are seeing good progress. Nor does the chart cover all interventions. There are many locally developed programmes (like Blackburn with Darwen's 'Vocabulary Box') that have been rigorously evaluated but are not yet available to schools outside the project or area, so are not included in the chart.

An example of a thoroughly evaluated programme is the highly effective 30-week Language4Reading small group intervention for nursery and Reception children, developed by the University of York with support from the Nuffield Foundation. This has the highest standard of scientific evidence behind it (a randomised controlled trial). The programme has now been developed in partnership with ICAN so that it is nationally available, under the name Nuffield Early Language Intervention.

Another very interesting intervention is Talk Boost, developed by The Communication Trust, the Every Child a Chance Trust and ICAN. This is a 10-week programme for small groups of four to seven year olds. Evaluation based on 'pre' and 'post' measures has shown strong impact. Children typically made 18 months progress on the test over the intervention period. Again, the programme has now been made widely available, with training and resources provided by ICAN.

Local authority and speech and language therapy teams in your area may already have particular intervention programmes for which they provide training, modelling and ongoing support. These may be the packages to go for, unless the staff delivering the interventions in your school are highly qualified in SLCN, and able to use and adapt 'off the peg' materials with little specialist support.

The good news is that Wave 2 language interventions can work. In an evaluation of the

Table 7.10 Wave 2 interventions for language

Early years	Key Stage 1 and 2	Secondary
*BLAST** (www.blastprogramme.co.uk) A small group programme designed to enhance and enrich the speech, language and communication skills of 3–4 year old children.		
*Nuffield Early Language Intervention Programme** (www.ican.org.uk) Two programmes that can be self-contained or used in sequence. The Nuffield Nursery Intervention is a 10-week group programme targeting narrative skills, vocabulary knowledge and listening skills. The Nuffield Reception intervention is a 20-week programme with a similar focus but a mix of group and individual sessions. During the final 10 weeks, the intervention includes training in phonological awareness and letter sound knowledge.		
*Talk Boost** (www.ican.org.uk/talkboost) A ten-week group programme for Reception and KS1. Aims to close the gap between language delayed children and their peers. Focuses on listening, vocabulary, sentence building, story-telling and conversations.		
Talk Volunteers (www.sheffield.gov.uk) Resources to support schools in setting up a Talk Volunteer programme for pupils who find it difficult to contribute to class discussion, or use talk that is very limited.		
	*Speak Out** and *Speech Bubble** (www.londonbubble.org.uk) Drama-based group interventions for children who lack confidence because they are learning EAL, have language delay or specific needs such as selective mutism or Asperger syndrome.	

Table 7.10 continued

Early years	Key Stage I and 2	Secondary
*Nursery Narrative** (Black Sheep Press) Activities to develop listening and expressive language through a narrative framework of 'Who' 'Where' 'When' and 'What happened next'. Nursery and YR.	*Key Stage I Narrative, Key Stage 2 Narrative** (Black Sheep Press) Activities that use a narrative framework to improve expressive language, attention and listening, and story-writing skills.	
Developing Baseline Communication Skills (Speechmark) For 4–5 year olds. Targets listening, comprehension, expression and social interaction.	*Speaking, Listening and Understanding* (Speechmark) For Y1 and 2. Targets a range of language functions such as following instructions, narrating, describing, explaining, predicting. *Understanding and using spoken language* (Speechmark) For Y3 and 4. Targets active listening and memory, thinking and reasoning, using language effectively.	
*Languageland** (Black Sheep Press) Nursery, YR and Key Stage I Activities target listening, sound awareness, vocabulary, comprehension and narrative skills.		
One Step at a Time (Network Continuum Education) A structured programme for the systematic teaching of spoken language skills for children aged 3 to 7. Based on four types of spoken language skill that are crucial for progress in school: conversation (nursery), listening (YR), narrative (Y1) and discussion (Y2). A whole-class programme but also suitable for intervention work.		
Teaching Talking (GL Assessment) Allows for screening and profiling children's language development, and provides activities and interventions to match profiled needs.		
	*Language for Thinking** (Speechmark) Provides a clear structure to help children's language develop from the 'here and now' to the 'how and why'. Suitable for KS1 children and older children with SEN.	

Table 7.10 continued

Early years	Key Stage 1 and 2	Secondary
	Let's Talk* (www.leicester.gov.uk) A Leicester-based training programme to enable a school team to run weekly language groups focusing on listening skills, vocabulary, narrative, sequencing, memory and reasoning.	
SPIRALS* (Routledge) Nursery through to early primary years. A structured approach based on small-group circle times. Develops attention, language, thinking and social communication skills.		
Time to Talk (LDA) A 40-session programme to develop oral and social interaction skills. YR and KS1.		
Talking Partners* (www.educationworks.org.uk) Foundation Stage to KS2. A structured 10 week group programme which targets a range of language functions such as listening to and following instructions, news telling, describing, comparing, analysing and reporting. Links closely to classroom literacy learning.		
	Nurturing Talk (www.educationworks.org.uk) Key Stage 1 to 3. For children with social, emotional and behavioural needs. Based on the Talking Partners programme and linked closely to SEAL materials. Develops speaking and listening skills in both a social and an academic context.	
	Talking Maths (Liverpool Local Authority) Y1 to 7. Develops speaking and listening skills in the context of the language of mathematics.	
	ELCISS Narrative Intervention Programme, ELCISS Vocabulary Intervention Programme* (www.elciss.com and Speechmark) Small group interventions to develop vocabulary and narrative skills, for 8- to 18-year-olds	
		Talking Partners @ Secondary* (www.educationworks.org.uk) A ten-week speaking and listening intervention programme based on the Talking Partners approach and covering a similar range of language functions.

Table 7.11 Social communication interventions

Early years	Key Stage 1 and 2	Secondary
*Social Thinking** (www.socialthinking.com) Develops children's ability to take in the thoughts, emotions and intentions of the people they are interacting with; teaches listening skills, the ability to hold a conversation, and inferential thinking.		
	*Social Communication Intervention Programme (SCIP)** (www.roundwaycentre.org.uk/Publications/SCIP) 1–1 intervention for children in Key Stage 1 and 2, which helps the child develop inference and social interaction skills.	
	Socially Speaking (LDA) For children aged 7–11, and older pupils with learning difficulties.	
		*Social Use of Language Programme** (GL Assessment) A group programme suitable for students aged 12 to 18+ years. For use by speech and language therapists, SENCOs and educational psychologists. Provides a framework within which to assess and develop students' communication, interpersonal and social skills.
		Talkabout (Speechmark) A resource for running social skills groups. Beginning with a basic assessment procedure to evaluate the student's self-awareness, as well as the awareness of others, it is divided into six levels: improving the awareness of self and others; allowing students to assess their own communication skills; taking the student through eight levels of body language; improving knowledge about how we talk; improving conversational and listening skills; awareness and use of assertiveness skills.

Table 7.11 continued

Early years	Key Stage 1 and 2	Secondary
Social Skills Programmes (Speechmark) Photocopiable session plans for different age groups ranging from early years to adolescence		
Comic Strip Conversations * (www.thegraycenter.org) 1–1 intervention in which an adult uses stick figures and symbols to help the child understand social situations, prepare them for future events or look at how they might have responded differently in situations where things went wrong.		
*Social Stories** (www.thegraycenter.org) 1–1 intervention which helps children understand and manage social situations through personalised stories about situations they have found problematic.		

BLAST programme, for example, children made on average nine months gain in six weeks on Sure Start language measures and the Reynell test, with progress maintained at follow up one year later. Children taking part in the well-known Talking Partners intervention made 18 months of progress, compared with 5 months for a control group, over ten weeks. Talk Boost, as we have seen, led to language gains seven times greater than would be expected through normal maturation. Primary narrative programmes have shown expressive language age increases of 14 months in a six-month period, and led to a reduction in the need for speech and language therapy referrals. Even at secondary age, interventions like ELCISS and Bolton's Talking Partners @ Secondary have been shown to make a real difference.

The following case studies offer some examples I saw of good practice in using Wave 2 interventions.

CASE STUDY

In Stoke-on-Trent, training is provided on the One Step at a Time programme and links into a system for accrediting practitioners' skills at four levels of expertise. Children in nursery and reception classes have their language skills assessed, and are identified as at 'green', 'amber' or 'red' according to the results.

All children take part in core elements of the programme – songs, stories and word of the week. Children at 'amber' have a small group session twice a week tailored to their needs. It might, for example, involve games in which children follow instructions with two key message elements. Children at 'red' take part in daily group sessions. Re-assessment following intervention has shown significant gains for all groups of children.

CASE STUDY

At St Bede primary in Bolton, children in the nursery are grouped for Nursery Narrative sessions. Over a twenty-week period they focus on the concepts of 'who', 'where', 'when' and 'what is it?'. Each concept has its own 'sign' to provide visual support.

A typical session might include a game like 'Pass the smile' to focus on the word 'who' ('*Who* will you pass your smile to?'), then a rehearsal of the rules for good listening, then passing round a bag of miniature family figures which the children delve into and describe, in response to the question '*Who* have you found in the bag?'.

Later, there might be a 'who is missing' hiding game using the same characters. The intervention programme feeds back into general planning for the setting; as a result of the groups staff realised, for example, that they needed to do more on prepositions with all children, so have now built this into their everyday practice.

CASE STUDY

In Bolton, the inclusion advisory teaching service provides training on the locally developed Talking Partners @ Secondary programme. Staff also model delivery in classroom settings. The intervention was originally designed to support learners with challenging behaviour, but it has also been successful for EAL learners and pupils with SLCN. The programme consists of a weekly one-hour group session and one or two follow-up sessions to consolidate the taught skills.

Visual frameworks are used to help students formulate ideas and structure their talk. Pupils might in the sessions tell and re-tell local and national news stories, for example, or undertake 'expert interviews', or develop their understanding of idioms. Evaluation of the pilot showed substantial gains on language assessments, on average six months' gain over ten weeks of intervention.

Summary

In this chapter we have considered a range of strategies to provide extra support to children whose speech, language or communication development gives cause for concern. This is only part of the picture, however. To be truly successful, strategies will also need to extend beyond the setting or school, and include the all-important home environment. In the next chapter we will look at some of the excellent practice in involving parents and carers that I saw in my time in post as Communication Champion.

Support for talk

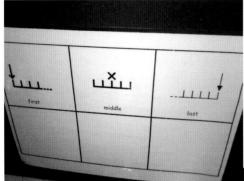

Visual support for concepts

Visual support: door labels

Visual support for everyday learning

Visual support: symbols

8 | Working with parents and carers to develop their children's language skills

Introduction

Some of the most effective work I saw in my time as Communication Champion was the support provided to parents to help them become skilled in developing their child's language and communication.

This really matters, because how parents interact with their children is such a powerful predictor of the child's language development and learning. As we saw in Chapter 2, in order to develop well, children need parents who tune in to their communications from the moment of birth, and respond in sensitive ways. We also know from the Effective Provision of Pre-school Education (EPPE) study that what is often called 'the home learning environment' in the pre-school years (frequency of being read to, going to the library, singing songs, learning poems and rhymes, plus the more obvious early learning activities like being taught letters and numbers) is a more powerful predictor of literacy attainment at age 11 than whether the child attended pre-school and the academic effectiveness of their primary school (see www.education.gov.uk/a0068162/effective-provision-of-pre-school-education-eppe).

Recent data from the Programme for International Student Assessment (Organisation for Economic Co-operation and Development, 2012) shows that, after controlling for socio-economic background effects, those pupils whose parents regularly read books to them when they were in the first year of primary school scored on average 14 points higher in reading tests at age 15 (the equivalent to about a quarter of a school year). Also important predictors were whether parents had talked about things they had done during the day or told stories to their children.

It wasn't only these language inputs when the child was young which mattered. There were also strong associations between reading attainment and parent–child activities at the time the student was 15 years old. The students who did better (again after controlling for social background) were those whose parents discussed political and social issues with them either weekly or daily, discussed books and films and TV programmes with them, or ensured that the family regularly ate a main meal together around a table.

Promotional strategies

One of my abiding memories from my time in post was a young mother who said to me, of her toddler, *'e don't talk to me, so I don't talk to 'im*. Nothing in her experience had ever told her that it is possible and indeed essential to talk to children before they are old enough to talk back.

Not all parents know how communication develops and how they can help. For example, surveys conducted during the national year of communication showed that only a quarter of parents knew that on average babies say their first words between 12 and 18 months. They knew much more about walking milestones than talking milestones. A fifth of parents-to-be believe it is only beneficial to communicate with their baby from the age of three months and one in twenty believe that communicating with their baby is only necessary when they are six months or older.

Yet there is definitely an appetite among parents for more knowledge. Speech and language therapists in one local area, for example, told me how when they provided information about the impact of indiscriminate television-watching under the age of two, and the prolonged use of dummies, the reaction from parents was 'No one told us this before.' Once given the facts, parents were all too happy to make changes to their interactions with their child.

Simple promotional strategies can be very effective in providing information and support to parents. These seem to work best when they provide a subtle 'nudge' to change behaviours, rather than a lecture. One of the most creative nudges I saw was in a pack produced by the National Deaf Children's Society for parents of very young deaf children. The pack includes an ingenious bib with a picture of a baby hiding their eyes and the words 'Let's Play Peek-a-boo' on one side, and the words 'Where's Baby?' with the same picture on the other – an absolute invitation to get into a game.

Another lovely example is in Wandsworth, where speech and language therapists have put 'Nappy chatter matters' posters with songs and rhymes in places where parents go to change their babies' nappies. In Nottinghamshire parents are given free height charts – guaranteed to be used – which include speech and language milestones. In Coventry, parents were given laminated 'Chatter cards' (ideas for chat while out and about) with a big ring that clips on the side of the buggy. For a similar purpose, a Buggy Buddies scheme devised in Hertfordshire for Walk to School Week provides parents with daily fun interactive activities, with certificates and stickers for completing them. And in Sheffield a huge, purple, room-height poster of 'Top tips for new parents' was displayed in the maternity hospital, so every new parent would see it; they were also given a miniature, pocket-sized version to keep.

Particularly useful websites for parents are ICAN's Talking Point (www.talkingpoint.org.uk), the National Literacy Trust's Words for Life site (www.wordsforlife.org.uk), and local sites like those of Worcestershire (www.worcestershire.gov.uk/slcnpathway). All have information about milestones, tips, and activities for different age groups. There are short films for parents on Hounslow's site (www.hounslow.gov.uk/index/education_and_learning/schools_and_colleges/speech_and_language/speech_language_videos.htm) and on that of The Communication Trust www.thecommunicationtrust.org.uk – search for 'Through the eyes of the child').

Also from The Communication Trust is *Small Talk,* a booklet full of lovely ideas for parents of under-fives, and two *Listen Up* activity packs (one for children from birth to age five, one for primary school-aged children), which suggest activities themed around the language development pyramid – interaction, play, listening and understanding.

There is also no shortage of local leaflets, produced by speech and language therapists and early-years practitioners, giving parents top tips on communication. Over the course of the national year of communication I saw hundreds; each one had its merits, but some of my favourite quick tips were these (Figure 8.1).

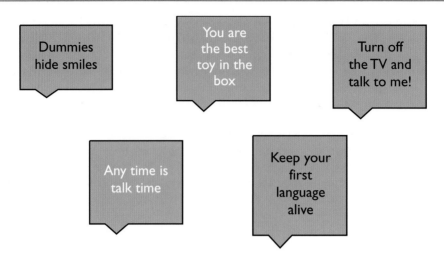

Figure 8.1 **Top tips for parents and carers**

For a bit more detail, my personal advice sheet for parents of children of all ages would be:

- Remember that you are the best toy in the box. For your child, nothing beats time spent talking and playing with you.
- Get right down to your child's level and make eye contact – even if this means lying on the floor.
- Think of it like tennis – serve and return – wait for your child to communicate, then respond.
- Keep dummies for sleep time – try walking round with a lolly in your mouth yourself for an hour, to experience the effect on conversation!
- Turn off the TV or radio when you are talking with your children, so they can really listen.
- Comment rather than ask lots of questions; instead of 'What's your favourite ice-cream?' try 'Mmm…ice-cream…I love vanilla flavour'.
- Add words to what your child says – so if they say 'Car gone', you could say 'Yes, the car's gone round the corner'.
- If they make mistakes, don't correct them but say it back to them the right form so they hear how it should sound.
- Share books with your child from their very earliest months, for as long as they still enjoy it – even nine year olds love to hear a chapter a night of a book that is just a bit too hard for them to read by themselves.
- Teach them to always ask if they haven't understood something or don't know the meaning of a word, so they will continue to build their language skills and vocabulary as they grow older.
- If English is not your home language, talk to your child in the language that feels most natural – you don't have to use English as they will pick this up quickly if they speak and understand their home language well. Don't worry if you mix languages when talking – that's fine too.

The 'Keep your own language alive' is a particularly important message. I came across many practitioners who misguidedly advised parents to speak to their child in English at home – whereas all research, as we saw in Chapter 2, shows that children's development in a second language is quicker and more secure if they have a solid foundation in their first language.

What works

Promotional strategies seem to work best where they involve the whole local children's work-force in conveying key messages about communication, and involve a 'layered' approach where support is offered to all but can be intensified according to need. Stoke Speaks Out, which we met in Chapter 1, is one such example of joining up. Another is Nottinghamshire's 'Language for Life' strategy;

CASE STUDY

In Nottinghamshire a community-wide 'Language for Life' strategy brings together speech and language therapists and other health staff, staff in Children's Centres and a range of local authority teams, from early years specialist teachers to school improvement services. Before a baby is born, their parents will have received information on commu-nication in ante-natal groups in Children's Centres, hospitals and clinics. At the newborn hearing screen, health staff give out leaflets about songs and rhymes. Later, the oral health team will give out information about dummies.

For the birth to two age range there are messages about communication at generic Children's Centre events such as baby massage and Stay and Play and specific language-focused Toddler Talk and Stay and Sign sessions.

The speech and language therapy service's Children's Centre core offer includes support for harder to reach families with 0–3 year olds. All Children's Centres have allo-cated therapy time, including capacity to visit at home families who do not respond to letters inviting them to make an appointment with the therapy service. Every Centre has a strategic Early Language Lead and a Home Talk Worker with enhanced training and support from a speech and language therapist.

All parents have the opportunity to talk through their child's language development at the Healthy Child Programme two-year development check led by health visitors. The check includes a parent-interview language screen, developed by speech and language therapists, with a 'traffic light' alert system which triggers any support needed, and the use of relevant advice leaflets. Children on 'red' (using less than ten words) are referred straight away to a speech and language therapist. Parents of children on 'green' (no concerns – using more than 30 words) are given and talked through a leaflet on 'Joining lots of words together'. Where children are on 'amber' (some concerns – using ten to 30 words) the health visiting team will talk them through a leaflet carefully chosen to match the child's needs – for example, one on Play if that seems to be an issue. They may also be referred to the Home Talk outreach worker for a six-week programme of home visits to model strategies for interaction.

The outcomes of the strategy are very positive. Communication, language and liter-acy scores on the Early Years Foundation Stage Profile have shown significant improvements year on year for all children, and as well as this there has been a closing of the gap; the difference in scores between the lowest achieving 20% of children and their peers is narrowing. Evaluation has shown that the Home Talk Worker package prevented language delay for 60% of a sample of two year olds, with the remaining 40% referred early for speech and language therapy.

Reaching harder-to-reach families

Sometimes it takes extra effort to make sure messages get to all families. I saw a good deal of ingenuity here in early-years services – like weaving information about language into workshops and groups that are a real 'draw' for parents, such as sleep and weaning, rather than holding language-specific events, and engaging dads by running an event where they were challenged to come in and build a den with their child, using materials provided.

In Stoke-on-Trent, there is an awareness that some parents may not find reading easy, so settings have recorded true/false questions about children's language development on Talking Tins to make an interactive quiz.

In Hillingdon, families waiting for appointments to see social workers or housing officers are given a small pack containing toys, a book to share and a top tip sheet about supporting their child's communication development. In Rotherham, leaflets promoting family learning courses are given out at taxi ranks, because that is where many fathers from harder-to-reach Asian families work.

In Cambridgeshire, speech and language therapists positioned themselves outside supermarkets to 'catch' parents of young children and get them to take part in a 'Trolley Challenge' of fun things to keep their child busy (and chatting) while doing the shopping.

In Milton Keynes, the early-years team worked with the local radio station, Heart FM, to air messages about communication, voiced by Mylene Klass.

For school-age children, what I saw working was engaging parents in non-threatening activities that appealed to their interests and their desire to give their child the best start in life. A group of schools in the town of Winsford in Cheshire, where deprivation levels are high and children's language and communication skills poor on entry to school, implemented an initiative called Talking Boxes. Children and their parents work together in school to decorate a sturdy wooden box which they then fill with objects that are special to the child. Each child has the opportunity to bring their box into class and tell everyone about their special things. The schools have found this a good way of getting parents to come into school. 'We would never have got them in for a workshop on language or reading to your child', they say. 'But decorating a box – everyone felt they could do that. It was safe.'

Babies

Recent research (Roulstone et al., 2011) has shown that children's language development at the age of two (their understanding and use of vocabulary and use of two- or three-word sentences) strongly predicts their performance on school entry assessments covering language, reading, maths and writing. 'Growing up in Scotland', a major study tracking children's development over time, has similarly found that seeds are sown very early: researchers found that progress in language between the ages of three and five was strongly predicted by language skills at age two. Particularly for children whose parents have no or lower qualifications, poor early communication skills are likely to persist.

To me this means that there is an urgent need to work with parents from pregnancy on, supporting them in developing their child's communication skills – looking, listening, turn-taking, imitation and gesture – through babyhood and the toddler period.

Some excellent practice I saw for this age group was a 'Baby Talk' group I watched in a Plymouth children's centre. Here, practitioners have been trained by the local speech and language therapy service to run weekly groups for parents of children around six months old. Parents are shown how to get right down to the baby's level, making eye contact and copying the baby's actions and signals. The resulting parent–baby 'conversations' I watched were amazing.

At a children's centre in North Yorkshire, parents bring their babies for a weekly session. At the heart of each session is 'the box' – a shallow box of ten objects, each with an associated song. The box is passed round and each baby is given time to choose an object. One little girl, Cassie, chooses a small wooden boat every time; when she chooses, the adults sing 'Row, row, row your boat'. The babies soon know what they like and know how to wait for their turn – listening, concentrating, knowing what is coming next, anticipating the actions in the songs. Then the box goes round again for another turn. After that the babies explore different treasure baskets; parents are encouraged to comment on what the baby is doing and wait for a response. They then share a book with their child, before the session ends with a song.

Amazingly, just as in Plymouth's Baby Talk groups, there is never any crying or fussing. The babies seem to know that they are leading the reciprocal 'dance' of communication, that the adults are fully tuned in and following their lead. The repetition of a familiar structure each week gives them security and enables them to predict and anticipate.

For some parents, home visits may be more appropriate than group sessions. In Wigan, I came across a very successful 'Baby and Tots Talk Service' staffed by midwives and a speech and language therapist. The team work with high-risk expectant mothers and parents of babies under six months. Risks include mental health difficulties, domestic violence, homelessness, learning difficulties, substance misuse and safeguarding issues.

The aim of the service is to increase parents' awareness of early communication, increase their confidence in interacting with their baby and help them use positive interaction strategies. The speech and language therapist visits parents in their own home to model and support parent/child interaction. Where children are in foster care, sessions are delivered during the birth parents' contact sessions with their baby at Children and Family Centres. The therapist also has an important role in helping parents to access other services such as parenting support and Children's Centre services.

Feedback from parents shows the impact this very early help can have:

- A father said that he had listened to the advice given at the initial assessment and talked to the baby while in the womb. He frequently repeated a term of endearment that he had chosen to use when speaking to the baby. Both parents reported that within the first 36 hours of delivery the baby started responding to this phrase, and continues to do so.
- Another father has responded well to advice about copying his baby's facial expression. He sits for minutes at a time, face to face with his baby, repeating his facial expression and waiting for his baby to respond.
- Following discussion and advice given at the initial assessment, during the second session (when the baby was four weeks old) a teenage mother said 'if you come close to them, that's when they see best. They put a face to the voice, kind of thing.'

Early years settings

Early years settings use a range of strategies to support parents' learning about language and communication:

- Stay and play sessions where adults can model good practice like watching, following the child's lead and commenting.
- Parent workshops or coffee mornings.
- Jointly assessing where children are in their language development.
- Newsletters and displays.

In one packaway setting practitioners set up a carousel of activities for parents to do with their children; on every table was an invitation to try out a particular strategy to promote language development. Staff stationed themselves on different tables and modelled these strategies.

A daycare setting in Torbay became involved in a local Every Child a Talker 'Dump the dummy' campaign, setting up a 'dummy tree' in the foyer for children to hang their dummies on in a small bag. Alongside the tree were leaflets for parents, and for the children a dummy fairy (who will take away the dummies from the tree to give them to very little children, leaving behind a small gift and letter in return). Comments from parents included 'Since giving up his dummy he talks more', and 'I've really noticed how his talking has come on. He's stringing sentences together.'

At Robin Hood primary school, the early language lead practitioner developed a nursery blog to encourage parents to support their child's language development. She uses the blog to describe what children have been doing in the nursery and (with parents' consent) posts photographs of activities. These have been a real draw, encouraging parents to access the school website. They were asked to look at the photographs with their children, using the blog as a starting point for conversation. Here is one extract from the blog:

Snow

We have had fun in the snow. We talked about how it felt, what it looked like and what clothes we needed to wear to keep us warm. The children enjoyed watching the 'snowman' video which you can find on You Tube. Watch the video together and talk about what is happening in the story.

Talking tip

Think about the different words you can use when talking about snow–
Cold, freezing, chilly, white, bright, soft, fluffy, icy, fluttering, crunchy, crisp

Books at bedtime

Children who have never had a story read to them, who never hear words that rhyme, who never imagine fighting with dragons or marrying a prince, have the odds overwhelmingly against them.

(Wolf, 2007)

As we have seen at the start of this chapter, whether parents read to their children is a significant predictor of later achievement. It also links to social mobility. Being read to at age five predicts whether a child brought up in poverty will themselves escape poverty as an adult (Blanden, 2006). It even predicts whether a child will have behaviour difficulties; one study (Ermisch, 2008) estimated that if half or all the five-year-old children who are read to less than daily were instead read to on a daily basis there would be a corresponding 10 per cent and 20 per cent reduction in the proportion of five-year-olds with social and emotional difficulties.

Early years settings have been highly creative in getting messages about bedtime reading across to parents. One setting made up 'bedtime bags' for children to take home using hot-water bottle covers as the container for a book or rhyme and story cards to sequence. At Norfolk primary school in Sheffield, staff organised a 'Book at bedtime' event with a mocked-up bedroom (a bed, blackout blind and curtains). Staff wore dressing gowns and modelled sharing stories. At Moorlands Centre nursery school in Milton Keynes, all staff (including the head teacher) wore their pyjamas and invited families to bring their children in their nightclothes. They heard about the history of bedtimes (including bedpans) from the head teacher, about good teeth-cleaning from the dental health team, then listened to bedtime stories read by staff. The children were then provided with hot milk while their mums and dads read to them.

One Every Child a Talker setting in Bournemouth targeted dads by organising a bedtime reading challenge. The practitioners put up posters and sent home leaflets saying 'Did you know that 80 per cent of fathers say they don't have time for bedtime stories these days – it can't be true here, can it?' They then supplied story sacks and disposable cameras, and set dads a challenge to read to their child, with great success.

A good source of resources for bedtime reading events is the Bookstart website (www.bookstart.org.uk), which has lovely posters, booklists and information leaflets for parents on how to share books with their child.

This aspect of 'how to' is important. I remember one parent survey undertaken during the national year of communication, where a number of parents said that when reading to children it was a bad thing if the child kept interrupting. So modelling how to read aloud in a lively and interactive way can make a big difference. A parent who watched a practitioner read aloud with intonation, for example, said 'I read to my child, but I don't change my voice like you do – I'm going to go home and try that.'

The ideas from dialogic book talk (see Chapter 4) also come in handy here. Booktrust's Bookstart Corner initiative supports children's centres in running an outreach home visiting programme which models dialogic book sharing for parents. Blackpool local authority used dialogic book talk as a key element of its 'Closing the gap' project, designed to enhance the life chances of children from hard to reach families. The project worked with severely disadvantaged two-year-old children and their families for a period of a year. Outreach workers made weekly home visits to families in the first term, reducing to fortnightly visits in the second term and monthly visits in the third term, modelling dialogic reading techniques and play interactions. Evaluation of impact showed that in spite of starting with very low baseline skills, children caught up in their understanding and use of vocabulary and showed a much increased ability to sit and pay attention for sustained periods.

Take-homes

It's all very well to tell parents to talk to their child – but many will wonder what on earth to talk about. It can feel awkward and difficult unless there is a focus.

The most successful practice I saw therefore involved providing parents and children with *something to talk about*, rather than a general message. Lots of settings, for example, have made and sent home 'Chatterboxes' – shoeboxes covered with wrapping paper and filled with objects to explore, perhaps a book, and ideas for things to do. These might be themed around a topic, such as the seaside, or birthdays, or a nursery rhyme. In Northumberland I saw a fabulous 'Twinkle Twinkle Little Star' box, containing the rhyme, a card star to thread with wool, a star finger puppet, a biscuit recipe and star cutter, and some glow-in-the-dark stars. In Hillingdon a Jack and Jill box had a bucket, vinegar, bandages, plasters and brown paper for parents and children to re-enact the rhyme together.

The boxes can be designed to focus on a particular aspect of language development. For example, a child just learning to use verbs might have a box themed around the word 'push', with objects like a toy car and small ramp to push the car up. Other boxes might encourage parents and children to imitate each other (a very important feature of early language learning), by for example having two rather than one of each musical instrument in a sound-making bag.

Ideally, tips for promoting children's language development will be linked to these specific take-home activities, so that parents can apply them in a meaningful context. In Warrington, for example, practitioners might pop a card saying 'Wait for your child to comment on these items BEFORE you do' inside a treasure box or story sack. In Hammersmith and Fulham, practitioners glue a list of key vocabulary linked to the activity on the inside of Chatterbox lids.

Other settings make a habit of sending home a visual story map of the key events in a story that has been shared in the setting, encouraging parents to ask their child to tell them the story at home. Scrapbooks and photo albums recording memorable events serve a similar purpose.

Another great idea is sending home a bag that contains everything a family needs to make a small, den-like space in their home (an 'adventure den', a 'sparkle den' and so on), with props to promote play and talk. Bags like these can be home-made, or are commercially available as part of Elizabeth Jarman's work on Communication Friendly Spaces™. Many practitioners also run events to help parents know how to make best use of these spaces. In Sheffield, for example, the Family Learning Service provide parents with Family Chatter Bags (Sparkle Den, Rainbow Den, Adventure Den, Music Den) alongside a six-week 'Talking together' course.

The primary and secondary years

So far, much of the good practice in this chapter has been about the early years. Certainly, this is a crucial phase in which to reach parents with messages about promoting communication. But as we saw earlier, parents' interactions with their children make a difference right through the age range. So what can schools do to support parents of older children?

One good idea is to put on the school's virtual learning environment a list of key vocabulary that children will soon be meeting in class, and suggest that parents pre-teach these words to their child. Lower Place primary in Rochdale uses this approach and has also taught EAL learners how to translate the words for their parents using Babblefish and Google.

I think it is also worth sharing with parents the messages from research about the links between attainment at school and factors such as eating together as a family, discussing films and TV programmes, and reading to children even when they can read themselves. Maybe some of the ideas from early years practice, such as workshops and 'Challenges', would be successful with older children too.

Parents may also welcome information on hot topics such as whether or how to limit their child's use of TV and computer games. There's some good guidance out there for parents on issues like TV and technology – for example, a 'Ten point plan for parents: how to use technology as an communication opportunity' on the website of the Communication Trust (www.thecommunicationtrust.org.uk/resources/resources/hello-campaign-resources/technology-factboxes.aspx), which has ideas like parent and child using the internet together to research what happened in the world on the day the child was born and compare it to the day the parent was born, talking about any similarities or differences, or getting the child to teach parents how to use an aspect of technology (good for learning how to give instructions).

Even more than parents of younger children, parents of this age group need a structure that gives them something engaging to talk about. Children in Key Stage 1, for example, can be given a sticker to wear, with a suggestion for their parents – 'Ask me what I'm proud of today', or 'Today I have learned about floating and sinking. Ask me to tell you about it.' Older children can construct their own messages and write them on stickers, or record them on Talking Tins.

Many schools are experimenting with 'talk homework'. The gold family activity booklets from the SEAL resources (www.sealcommunity.org) are a rich source of ideas for activities that prompt discussion. Here are some ideas:

- Loves and hates.
- When are the times when you get on best as a family... and fall out?
- Talk about your dream home.
- Can you remember the day that I was born?
- The best/worst thing that happened to me today was...
- What cheers you up when you feel down?

At Sir Philip Howard Catholic primary school in Hatfield, ideas for talk homework (such as 'If you were a famous person who would you want to be?', and 'What was the best day out you ever had?') go up on the school website each week. Children then have time to discuss the question in class at the end of the week.

Other useful resources are Fink (Family Interaction Nurtures Kids) conversation starters card packs (www.finkcards.com), and a *Summer Talk* booklet that can be downloaded from the Communication Trust's website, full of ideas for family interaction and conversation during the summer holidays, including activities for long car journeys.

Summary

As we have seen in this chapter, much excellent practice exists in working with parents and carers of children and young people at risk of language delay, to get across messages about the practical, everyday steps they can take to encourage language development in the home. Care needs to be taken, however, to distinguish the needs of these parents from those of parents of children with the more severe biologically based special needs in speech, language and communication. Although the strategies discussed here are useful for all children, they are not likely to remedy the more persistent, in-built SLCN experienced by one in ten children. These children require 'Wave 3' provision, and different types of parental involvement. It is to this that we now turn, in the final chapter of this book.

Supporting children with more severe needs

In my time as Communication Champion I often had the chance to listen to young people with SLCN taking about the types of support they had had, and what they thought about it. Figure 9.1 shows a few of the illuminating things they said. What came across most clearly was their need to have choice in the support they received, and for support to work through natural systems like friendships, rather than paid 'minders.'

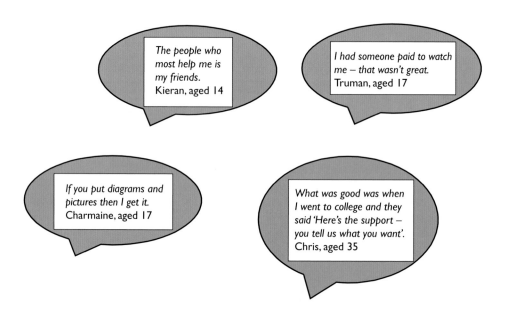

Figure 9.1 **What young people say about support**

Another very useful experience for me was a set of case studies of effective Wave 3 support for children and young people with SLCN which I commissioned from the charities which make up The Communication Trust. The following case studies provide some examples.

CASE STUDY: JOSH'S STORY

All seemed to be going well for Josh. He learned to sit, crawl and at the expected time. He said his first word at 18 months. However, by the time he was three and a half, he still had only a few single words and signs and so was referred to his local speech and language therapy service by the health visitor.

A month later, Josh had an initial speech and language assessment, which showed that his comprehension was within normal limits, but his ability to express his thoughts was very much delayed. At this point, much to his parents' concern, the practitioners at Josh's pre-school reported that they had observed some inappropriate behaviour from Josh and put it down to his difficulties initiating and joining in with play as he could not get his message across.

Josh's mother was delighted that shortly after his assessment he was offered a block of group therapy sessions to which she and his pre-school setting key worker were also invited. Josh's mother says that 'We learned a lot from watching the therapist play with Josh and it gave us both ideas to try with him to get him talking more.'

In the meantime, two members of staff from Josh's pre-school took part in Elklan training, which allowed them to improve the communicative environment of Josh's preschool. A speech and language therapist visited the preschool to deliver Makaton signing training to all the staff and to Josh's parents.

Josh's spoken vocabulary has increased, albeit at a slower rate than expected, but he began to use a range of signs effectively. Importantly, this reduced frustration for both Josh and his family.

A Common Assessment Framework (CAF) meeting was set up so that professionals were able to liaise on the future needs of Josh and his family. As a result, Josh was assessed by an educational psychologist and a consultant paediatrician, to investigate his overall development. A special transition meeting was arranged by the local authority early-years inclusion adviser, to ensure that appropriate support would be in place when Josh started at mainstream school.

CASE STUDY: ROSE'S STORY

Rose is ten years old, and has learning difficulties and complex communication difficulties. She attends her local mainstream school. She was not making satisfactory progress or experiencing an inclusive education as she was increasingly withdrawn from the class to work one to one with her teaching assistant on Individual Education Plan targets.

Then the school bought in some speech and language therapy time to support Rose. In addition to providing one-to-one therapy to Rose for half an hour every two weeks, the speech and language therapist provided training to the teaching assistant and the class teacher. She also advised on classroom strategies to enable Rose to access lessons. The therapist was given half an hour every two weeks to work with the class teacher and assistant. A monthly communication meeting with Rose's parents, the therapist and school staff was also established.

The therapist introduced the school staff to a symbol supported curriculum to help Rose record her work and recommended particular supportive software packages. Rose responded well to their use.

The monthly meetings helped to set more realistic and attainable targets for Rose so that she could experience the feeling of success. Both parents and school are clear about the targets and on how to help Rose achieve them so she experiences consistency of approach.

As a result of the coordinated support she now receives, Rose is now spending most of her time successfully learning in the mainstream classroom, and progressing up the P-scales.

CASE STUDY: JASON'S STORY

Jason is 17 and has Aperts syndrome, which is a complex craniofacial condition. He has a moderate visual disability, finds it difficult to hold a pen and is unable to write independently. His severe speech disability makes it difficult for him to be understood.

Jason's communication needs were assessed by a specialist teacher and an alternative communication plan was put in place. Initially, Jason was provided with a communication book, consisting of pages of picture symbols arranged in category areas. He was taught how to indicate his needs by pointing to pictures on a page. It became evident that Jason had the capability to develop more literacy and communication skills. Trials were undertaken with a range of electronic devices.

At first Jason used a simple picture based aid, but he later progressed onto a more sophisticated symbol based system. Ultimately he was able to use a device based on letter spelling and word prediction.

Jason had been frustrated at not being able to articulate fully his thoughts, feelings and wishes. He experienced isolation from his peers and a reduction in his personal autonomy. His communication aid made an enormous difference. Jason explains:

> I met a specialist teacher in communication who assessed me for a communication aid which spoke the words I needed to say. It was great! Suddenly people started to understand me and I could ask for things I needed independently.

The school set up a communication team to support Jason, made up of the specialist teacher, a speech and language therapist, and teaching assistants who were trained in the basics of using the communication aids (particularly in the programming, maintenance and technical aspects of the device).

Jason was provided with regular, additional teaching and training: one-to-one support for one hour each week with a specialist teaching assistant (working under the direction of the specialist teacher), and one hour each month one-to-one with the specialist teacher who monitored and evaluated his progress and set targets.

A clear recording system was put in place with SMART (specific, measurable, achievable, realistic and timed) targets. Jason was encouraged to participate in the setting of these targets which were presented in a child friendly and accessible way, with a sticker style reward card.

Jason was actively involved in recording his learning. He produced his own record of achievement which included a DVD showing progress and a magazine-style Record of Achievement which also acted as a transition document as he moved throughout the school and interacted with other professionals. Very importantly, opportunities were provided for Jason to meet with other people who used assistive communication in order to provide role models and support.

Jason's family and key workers were provided with training in the use of the technology. Jason's writing skills were also assessed and it was decided to introduce a laptop computer with specialist word predictive software. Over time Jason developed his skills to the extent whereby he was able to write independently, use word prediction and access all multimedia functions such as email and text.

Unfortunately, good practice like the examples in these case studies is not always evident. I came across many examples of poor practice – children waiting months or years for speech and language therapy assessment, children being refused communication aids on the grounds of cost, children whose teachers were unable to access specialist advice, young people who told me that 'If they hear you have a disability they treat you in a patronising way.'

Some of the poor practice, sadly, was in the classroom and reflected lack of knowledge by class and subject teachers. When the 2011 national year of communication was launched in Parliament, a parent spoke about the help provided for her twelve-year-old son James, who uses an electronic communication aid. This parent had received comments from teachers like 'I don't have anything to do with his lesson planning or homework, I leave that to the support assistant'; 'James doesn't use his talker in class – he has a tendency to press the buttons and the noise it makes is a distraction, so we keep it in the cloakroom during the day'; and 'Yes, I know his chair is on its own at the back of the class, but he really doesn't spend any time in class now; he just doesn't understand what we are learning about'.

We need to do better than this. So what are the key features of good practice at Wave 3? I think they are:

- Good training for class, subject teachers and teaching assistants.
- Appropriate classroom environment and teaching styles.
- Access to appropriate technology and use of signs and symbols.
- Support which promotes independence and support from friends and other pupils rather than dependence on adults.
- Social supports for the child – putting them in touch with others with similar needs.
- Full, equal partnership with the child's parents/carers, including making sure they have the information they need.
- Information for everyone who comes into contact with the child about how to communicate with them, for example through the use of Communication Passports.
- Really well supported transition as children move from early years to primary, primary to secondary and secondary to further education settings or work.
- Access to specialist advice from advisory teachers and speech and language therapists, with a strong partnership approach between specialists and school staff.

Some of the types of *training* on SLCN available have already been flagged up in this book – the Inclusion Development Programme, Elklan, Language for Learning, Hanen's Learning

Language and Loving It. Training for teaching assistants may also need to include training on how to use questioning appropriately, and how to scaffold children's talk and thinking. This is because of research comparing the language used by teaching assistants and teachers (Blatchford *et al.*, 2012). Broadly, the research found find that teachers tend to use 'opening up' language, whereas teaching assistants tend to use 'closing down' strategies. They give this example:

> Teaching assistant: When you're working I'll explain. Matthew, are you writing the names down? Have you put isosceles on there? Right. Can you write there isosceles triangle? OK boys. Right, Sian. Sit up, sit up.

The emphasis is on closed questions, keeping children on task, and completing tasks rather than learning. In contrast, a typical example of a teacher-led exchange opens up a topic, ensuring that all children have a chance to participate.

Teacher:	What do you think a whole number might be?
Jim:	It might be something that hasn't got any left, hasn't got like halves in it.
Teacher:	OK, that's a good idea. What about Ros's group? What do you think?
Ros:	We think it might be a fraction that goes into...
Teacher:	So you think it's a number that can be multiplied by itself? Fantastic. OK, Amy – you had an idea?
Amy:	We thought that one, two, three... That could...
Ruka:	If it had no zero at the end, like a thousand...
Teacher:	Aaah, fantastic. Oh, I see, you are thinking of a whole number without the W. So that sort of hole. So you think it's a number that looks like it might have a hole in it, like a zero, like an eight, like a six. Yes? Very interesting. Well. Ruka was the first person who got it right. So can you tell me what you think it might be?

Teachers also treat errors differently. While teaching assistants in general correct mistakes, teachers often withhold correction and scaffold children's thinking with further questions and hints. This helps children use complex language structures and vocabulary to explore, hypothesise, predict, explain, justify and check rather than just describe or report.

Appropriate *classroom environments* and *teaching styles* have been very well described by ICAN in two excellent checklists (primary and secondary) for parents of children with SLCN to use when choosing a school for their child. You can find these in the parents' section of the Talking Point website (www.talkingpoint.org.uk). The checklists suggest that parents look, for example, at whether staff use non-verbal communication to support what they are saying (gesture, pointing, even signing), whether there are careful seating arrangements which allow the child with SLCN to sit near the front facing the teacher, for example tables placed in a horseshoe shape or tables that can be easily moved around, whether all pupils are encouraged to ask questions and seek clarification. I thoroughly recommend these checklists to SENCOs, to help them take stock of the environment and teaching styles in classes that pupils with SLCN will be attending, and identify adaptations (reasonable adjustments)that may be needed

Access to appropriate technology, signs and symbols is vital. This is a growing and ever-changing field, so settings and schools need good advice (for example, from sources such as the ACE centres in Oldham and Oxford) on what is available – from iPad apps to highly sophisticated eye-gaze communication aid systems. It's also vital to ensure consistency in signs and symbols across the different settings a child may spend time in (home, school, clubs, health and short break settings). Springwater special school in North Yorkshire, for example, has a high proportion of pupils who are non-verbal or at a very early stage in communication development and is developing consistency by defining a 150-keyword vocabulary, divided into categories such as food, questions, and social words, then looking at how the vocabulary can best be represented in objects of reference, symbol and sign. This vocabulary is taught in a standardised way in schools and used by parents, healthcare workers and respite carers.

The use of technology, signs and symbols is one aspect of support which *promotes independence*. But it is also important to consider how the school can foster 'natural' forms of support such as that provided by friends and other pupils, rather than the traditional Velcro teaching assistant model of support which we know often isolates children from their peers and fosters dependence on adults.

Students also need opportunities to spend time (on line or face to face) with *others who have needs similar to themselves*. I was inspired, for example, by my experience of attending a residential weekend which was organised by the One Voice charity and brought together young people from across the country who use communication aids. One Voice also pair younger children with teenagers and young adults who mentor them and act as powerful role models.

Full, equal partnership with the child's parents/carers is key to children's success in school, and there is no better model here than the systems used in the national Achievement for All programme, in which parents are involved in regular 'structured conversations' in which the class teacher or form tutor really listen to their hopes and aspirations for their child. I also saw really good practice in schools which included parents as partners in any specialist training on SLCN provided to school staff, and in speech and language therapy services which empower parents to support their child's language development through, for example, the parent-child interaction video interaction programme devised by therapists in Camden and Islington, or the Hanen programmes like It Takes Two to Talk and Target Words.

Information for everyone who comes into contact with the child about how to communicate with them is essential. Communication Passports (see www.communicationpassports.org.uk for lovely examples, and www.callcentresscotland for a suggested framework) are one way of providing this information. Communication Passports can be laminated books, small pocket photo albums with text and photos inserted, or photocopied sheets. They provide a profile of the child or young person – their name and what they like to be called, important things about them, things that make them happy and how they show this, things that may upset or frighten them and how they show this, what they need to help them understand what others are saying, how they communicate and what motivates them.

Communication Passports can form part of *systems to support transition* as children move from early years to primary, primary to secondary and secondary to further education settings or work. The charity Afasic is the leader here with transition groups in a number of local areas, and specific publications to support transition. There is also a bank of very useful ideas in a report for the Communication Trust (Ayre and Roulstone, 2009).

Finally, to me the most important element of all in Wave 3 support is *access to specialist advice* from *advisory teachers* and *speech and language therapists*, with a *strong partnership* approach between specialists and school staff. Specialist advice may come from local authority advisory teams, from special schools, or in the form of outreach from teachers in resource bases in mainstream schools. In the next section I will explore the specialist role of the speech and language therapist, and describe some of the excellent ways I have seen schools work with their local therapy service to get the best from the available provision.

Working with speech and language therapists

'The waiting list is so long I don't see any point in referring.'

'Fantastic service – we see our speech and language therapist in school regularly.'

'We've so many children needing to see a therapist – there's no way she can ever see them all.'

These are just a few of the comments I heard in my time as Communication Champion. They reflect the huge variability in the way speech and language therapists are funded, and the priority given to this area by NHS and local authority commissioners. The historical disparities in funding are stark; I came across one London borough which had just two speech and language therapists for mainstream schools, for example, whereas a very similar borough nearby had fifteen.

In these circumstances, it is important to know how to get the best from whatever provision is available. To do so, we need to draw on research on the effectiveness of speech and language therapy, and the conditions in which their work can have the most impact.

What do we know?

There is certainly evidence that therapy can transform children's speech, language and communication, with the greatest effect on speech problems (including stammering) and expressive language. There is less evidence that therapy, *at least as it is currently provided* (often in blocks of around six weekly sessions), is effective for children with language comprehension difficulties.

The frequency, intensity and duration of therapy seems to be important. A study in which therapists saw four year old children in a group once a week for four hours at a time, over eight months, did show success in improving language comprehension. And a major piece of research in Scotland (McCartney et al., 2011) found that therapy delivered by well-trained and supervised speech and language therapy assistants (in this case, psychology graduates) three times a week in school, for 30–40 minutes each session over a fifteen-week period, was more effective for primary-aged children with expressive language problems than the much less intensive clinic-based therapy routinely provided by speech and language therapists. Group intervention provided by the assistants or therapists was just as effective as one-to-one sessions.

Another study used specialist teaching assistants – again working under the direction of speech and language therapists – to provide four, one-hour sessions a week for four to seven year olds, with good success.

Parents, as well as therapy assistants or teaching assistants, can be highly effective. Several research overviews show no difference between 'direct' (speech and language therapist) and 'indirect' (parent-administered) therapy for children with speech disorders and expressive language difficulties, where therapist and parents worked collaboratively to support the child.

Other evidence suggests that (except of course for children with severe or profound and multiple learning difficulties) children's level of nonverbal cognitive ability makes no difference to the progress they make in therapy. This calls into question the assumption sometimes made that therapy should be reserved for those with specific language impairment (poor language but normal non-verbal ability).

Training

Finally, there is a lot of evidence that high-quality training delivered by speech and language therapists to practitioners and teachers can be highly successful. The Every Child a Talker programme, for example, has shown that professional development for staff in early years settings, combined with careful tracking of children's progress, results in a reduction of up to 40 per cent in the proportion of children with language delay. In a project in Derbyshire, in which a therapist delivered training and coaching to early-years practitioners, children as a result showed an average increase of 26 per cent on standardised tests of language comprehension and 25 percentile points in expressive language.

In the primary school, speech and language therapists working in classrooms with teachers in Worcestershire have succeeded in reducing the percentage of children with severe listening and attention difficulties from 21 to 4 per cent, and significantly improving children's vocabulary of new topic words taught in class.

Implications for schools

All this evidence challenges some assumptions about how therapy should be provided, particularly assumptions held by parents. For them, the goal is often one-to-one direct therapy delivered by a specialist. In fact, with the exception of children with complex needs, a collaborative approach with highly trained assistants supervised by speech and language therapists, and able to deliver intensive therapy in school, may be more effective. Similarly, intervention may not necessarily have to be one-to-one. And the training that school staff receive – teachers as well as teaching assistants – is vital.

There may therefore be a need to work with your local therapy service to explore models of practice that allow for a team approach. The case study below provides an example.

CASE STUDY

In North Somerset, the local authority funds four therapy assistants and two days of speech and language therapy time. The assistants are hosted and line-managed by a local primary school. The therapy service coordinates all referrals, assesses children and trains and supervises the assistants. Children receive therapy for ten week blocks, two to three times a week in school. Additionally, the programme has trained 80+ learning support assistants in SLCN, so that they can continue to work with children when the specialist assistants have moved on. An outcome measure used for every child's programme shows that intervention is consistently meeting 90–95 per cent of targets set.

Having a specialist-trained teaching assistant or assistants in school makes a huge difference. I came across a number of local areas which had developed a strategy to provide intensive, accredited training (such as Elklan courses) to school-based teaching assistants, so that they could work under the direction of speech and language therapists to provide intervention programmes. In another effective partnership model, I saw some speech and language therapy services deliver a block of therapy in school for a half term, with the school's teaching assistant sitting in. The next block is then delivered by the teaching assistant.

Parents may well be suspicious of anything less than direct therapy from a speech and language therapist. We need therefore to provide them with the evidence on what works. It may help to use a simple analogy. You can explain that it is a bit like learning a foreign language – yes, it is helpful to have regular 'lessons' from an expert, but it is also vital that you have the right support from those with whom you are in everyday contact – from people, for example, who know that it won't help you if they gabble fast or speak louder, but that they need to speak to you in short, simple sentences, repeating what you say in correct form if you make mistakes, or taking what you say and repeating it back to you with one or two words added, to help you build longer sentences.

Such examples make clear to parents that the key element of the effective SLCN provision for their child will be the team approach, involving themselves, SLT, class teacher and teaching assistant, so that is how you have planned your SLCN provision in school – as in the example below.

CASE STUDY

At St Michael's primary in Cornwall, much has changed over the past six years, since a SENCO new to the role and a new speech and language therapist resolved to develop a team approach. At the time, children with SLCN were seen by therapists in a clinic setting, so there was little opportunity for collaboration and a backlog of referrals waiting for appointments. As part of an initiative to develop collaborative practice with schools which had high numbers of children on therapists' caseloads, the therapist ran an Elklan course for teaching assistants, teachers and parents, for two hours a week over ten weeks. Later, she provided Language for Learning training. The school fund an assistant for ten hours a week to work on SLCN every afternoon – working with children and making resources. The therapist supported her initially for one session a week for half a term, modelling work with a child while the assistant watched, then gradually handing over.

The SENCO also has a vital role. Where parents or teachers raise concerns about a child, she observes children in class, discusses them with their teachers, and undertakes some assessment using the Renfrew Action Picture Test, the British Picture Vocabulary Scale and the Word finding Vocabulary Test and an articulation assessment from Language for Learning. She shares the results with parents and teachers, and then will then either record that there are no concerns, discuss with the speech and language therapist, or make a formal referral to the therapist. Where children are referred, and the assessment shows that intervention is needed, a goal sheet is completed and shared with parents, teaching assistants and teachers. There are a number of support options (Figure 9.2).

Evidence of impact is provided through repeated RAG ratings of the severity of children's difficulties (red = severe, yellow = mild, green = no concerns), so as to show the movement of children between categories.

The results have been impressive. *All* children who were identified in Reception as in need of support from the speech and language therapy service have been successfully removed from the caseload before entering Key Stage 2, for example, unless they have Statements of SEN. Literacy and behaviour difficulties have been prevented. Staff report confidence in identifying and supporting children with SLCN, and parents – most importantly – feel that their children's needs are being met.

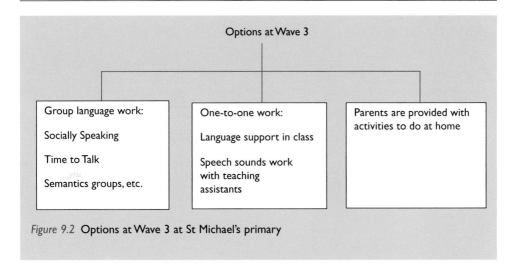

Figure 9.2 Options at Wave 3 at St Michael's primary

SENCOs will also want to work with class and subject teachers to stress their vital role in the partnership with specialists. They should, for example, seek to incorporate speech and language therapy targets into the child's day-to-day classroom experience. As an example, if a child's therapy target is to learn to use question words, such as 'what', a class or subject teacher might plan in a plenary to model the questions 'What did you do?' and 'What did you find out?' and then have the child put the questions to each group in turn.

Buying in additional time from speech and language therapists

An increasing number of schools are now buying in additional time from therapy services, as in the examples from Lewisham and Waltham Forest below. What I saw working well here was when the contract is for work at all three Waves – providing whole-staff training, supporting key staff to run Wave 2 interventions services and working with parents rather than simply 'treating' children at Wave 3.

CASE STUDY

In Lewisham, three schools part-funded enhanced speech and language therapy support to assess children, provide direct intervention to individuals and groups, help parents to use home programmes, run parent workshops and support teaching staff in implementing school programmes. The therapist also provided training to school staff, supported teachers in modifying the curriculum to meet children's needs and helped the schools to set up and run language booster groups in the Foundation Stage and Key Stage 1. As a result of successful early intervention, there has been a reduction in the therapist's caseload in Key Stage 2, and a year on year fall in the numbers of children identified by the schools as having persistent SLCN. There has also been a six-fold increase in the number of parents/carers involved with the provision for their child. Following presentations at SENCO meetings, other local school clusters are now buying in the enhanced service.

CASE STUDY

In Waltham Forest, schools have commissioned an enhanced speech and language therapy service to all mainstream primary schools. The service includes:

- working with class teachers to develop the listening and attention skills of the whole class;
- supporting schools to identify children with difficulties by offering classroom observations, screening assessments, and teacher/teaching assistant drop in sessions;
- training support staff to run language stimulation and language for thinking groups from Reception up to Year 6;
- organising accredited training for support staff;
- providing teaching staff with strategies for supporting children within the classroom setting; and
- running coffee mornings, drop in sessions and training workshops for parents.

External evaluation undertaken by a nearby university has shown significant improvements in children's language skills, as rated by their teachers and as assessed on standardised tests.

CASE STUDY

The majority of secondary mainstream and special schools in Hackney, as well as academies, a pupil referral unit and several colleges buy time from the local speech and language therapy team. Each institution commissions one to three days a week of therapy time. Typically, the schools have initially requested a traditional model of assessment and withdrawal work, but over time this has broadened to include training and work at whole-class level. One academy, for example, identified two science classes with high numbers of students with language and/or behaviour difficulties. The therapist worked in class on a rotation model in which she led one activity focusing on vocabulary and asking questions, the teacher led another, and a teaching assistant a third, with groups of students moving from one activity to the next every twenty minutes. This has been developed so that therapists now routinely work in class across a range of subjects on class models which include rotations, joint presentations with the teacher, and small group work. The therapist input includes working on self-help strategies, vocabulary and social communication skills.

Summary

This chapter has focused on working with outside agencies, and on support for children with persisting SLCN – on Wave 3 support.

Effective support at Wave 3 is the final element in a whole-school (or setting) approach. It builds on good conditions for language development at Wave 1 in the form of a place to talk, reasons to talk and teaching talking, and on good support for those who need it through inclusive classroom teaching and extra Wave 2 interventions.

It is this whole-school, three-wave approach which I saw working so effectively in a number of inspirational schools and settings, in my time as Communication Champion. It is these schools and settings which are making sure that their students leave them ready for a twenty-first-century future in which the ability to communicate will become ever more vital, and in which difficulties in communication become ever more disabling.

The purpose of this book, my last 'championing' activity, has been to spread this inspirational practice. I very much hope that it will do its job and that the whole-school approach will in time become the norm, for all children and young people.

References

Ainscow, M., Gallannaugh, F. and Kerr, K. (2012) *An Evaluation of the Communication Trust's 'Talk of the Town' Project, 2011–12*. Manchester: Centre for Equity in Education, University of Manchester.

Akerman, R. and Neale, I. (2011) *Debating the Evidence: An International Review of Current Situation and Perceptions*. Reading: CfBT.

Alexander, R. (ed.) (2009) *Children, Their World, Their Education: The Cambridge Primary Review*. London: Routledge.

Ayre, A. and Roulstone, S. (2009) *Transition to Secondary School: Supporting Pupils with Speech, Language and Communication Needs*. London: the Communication Trust.

Barton, G. (2011) Word-rich rule the world. *Times Educational Supplement*, 16 September.

Beck, I., McKeown, M. and Kucan, L. (2002) *Bringing Words to Life: Robust Vocabulary Instruction*. New York: Guilford Press.

Bennett, J. (2003) *Teaching and Learning Science*. London: Continuum.

Bercow, J. (2008) *Bercow Review of Services for Children and Young People (0–19) with Speech, Language and Communication Needs*. London: DCSF.

Biemiller, A. (2007) The influence of vocabulary on reading acquisition. *Encyclopedia of Language and Literacy Development*, 15 February. Available at http://literacyencyclopedia.ca/index.php?fa=items.show&topicId=19 (accessed 28 December 2012).

Biemiller, A. (2011) Vocabulary: what words should we teach? *Better: Evidence Based Education*, Winter: 10–11.

Bindon, R. (2006) *Tactical Teaching: Speaking and Listening*. Belmont, Western Australia: Steps Professional Development.

Blanden, J. (2006) *Bucking the Trend – What Enables Those Who are Disadvantaged in Childhood to Succeed Later in Life?* London: Department for Work and Pensions.

Blatchford, P., Russell, A. and Webster, R. (2012) *Reassessing the Impact of Teaching Assistants: How Research Challenges Practice and Policy*. London: Routledge.

Bos, C. and Anders, P. (1990) Effects of interactive vocabulary teaching on the vocabulary learning and reading comprehension of junior reading-disabled students. *Learning Disability Quarterly*, 13: 31–42.

Bronfenbrenner, U. (1994) Who cares for the children? In H. Nuba, M. Searson and D. L. Sheiman (eds), *Resources for Early Childhood: A Handbook*. New York: Garland.

Bryan, K. (2008) Speech, language and communication difficulties in juvenile offenders. In C. Hudson (ed.), *The Sound and the Silence: Key Perspectives on Speaking and Listening and Skills for Life*, 52–60. Coventry: Quality Improvement Agency.

Cassels, J. and Johnstone, A. (1985) *Words that Matter in Science*. London: The Royal Society of Chemistry.

Christakis, D., Zimmerman, F., DiGuiseppi, D. and McCarty, C. (2004) Early television exposure and subsequent attentional problems in children. *Pediatrics*, 113(4): 708–713.

Clegg, J., Leyden, J. and Stackhouse, J. (2011) *Evaluation report of the ICAN Secondary Talk Programme*. Sheffield: University of Sheffield. Available at www.ican.org.uk/secondarytalk.

Close, R. (2004) *Television and Language Development in the Early Years: A Review of the Literature.* London: National Literacy Trust.

Cohen, N., Barwick, M., Horodezky, N., Vallance, D. and Im, N. (1998) Language achievement, and cognitive processing in psychiatrically disturbed children with previously unidentified and unsuspected language impairments. *Journal of Child Psychology and Psychiatry,* 39: 865–877.

Conti-Ramsden, G., Durkin, K., Simkin, Z. and Knox, E. (2009) Specific language impairment and school outcomes: identifying and explaining variability at the end of compulsory education. *International Journal of Language and Communication Disorders,* 44(1): 15–35.

Croydon Local Authority (2011) *Developing Talk for Learning 2010/11.* London: Croydon Local Authority.

Cummins, J. (2000) *Language, Power and Pedagogy: Bilingual Children in the Crossfire.* Cleveden: Multilingual Matters.

Cummins, J. (2008) BICS and CALP: Empirical and Theoretical Status of the Distinction. In B. Street and N. H. Hornberger (eds), *Encyclopaedia of Language and Education, Volume 2: Literacy,* 2nd edn, pp. 71–83. New York, NY: Springer.

Cunningham, A. and Stanovitch, K. (1991) Tracking the unique effects of print exposure in children. *Journal of Educational Psychology,* 83: 264–274.

Desforges, C. and Abouchar, A. (2003) *The Impact of Parental Involvement, Parental Support and Family Education on Pupil Achievements and Adjustment: A Literature Review.* London: DfES.

DfE (2011) *Supporting Families in the Foundation Years.* London: DfE.

DfE (2012) *Special Educational Needs in England, January 2012: Statistical First Release.* London: DfE.

Elliott, N. (2009) *An Exploration of the Communication Skills of Unemployed Young Men.* Presentation at 'Locked In and Locked Out – Communication is the Key', Royal College of Speech and Language Therapists' conference, Cardiff, 19 November.

Ermisch, J. (2008) Origins of social immobility and inequality: parenting and early child development. *National Institute Economic Review,* 5(1): 62–67.

Feinstein, L. and Duckworth, K. (2006) *Development in the Early Years: Its Importance for School Performance and Adult Outcomes.* London: Centre for Research on the Wider Benefits of Learning.

Fenton, C. (2012) *TES Magazine,* 6 July.

Genesee, F. (1994) *Educating Second Language Children.* Cambridge: Cambridge University Press.

Gershon, M. (2012) Perfect the art of conversation. *TES Magazine,* 21 September.

Greenfield, N. (2007) Testing 1, 2, 3. Can you hear me? *Times Educational Supplement Scotland,* 19 October.

Gross, J. (2002) *Language Skills and Attainment.* Unpublished report. Bristol: Bristol Local Education Authority.

Hank, N. and Deacon, S. H. (2008) Building vocabulary in high poverty children. *Literacy Today,* 54: 29.

Hardman, E., Smith, F. and Wall, K. (2001) *An Investigation of the Impact of the National Literacy Strategy on the Learning of Pupils with Special Educational Needs in Mainstream Primary Schools: A Report to the Nuffield Foundation.* Newcastle: University of Newcastle upon Tyne.

Hart, B. and Risley T. (2003) The early catastrophe: the 30 million word gap by age 3. *American Educator,* 27(1): 4–9.

Hirsch, F. (1996) *The Schools We Need and Why We Don't Have Them.* New York: Doubleday.

Jordan, E. and Hayden, S. (2007) *Language for Learning.* London: Routledge.

Jordan, E. and Hayden, S. (2011) *Language for Learning in the Secondary School.* London: Routledge.

Kispal, A. (2008) *Effective Teaching of Inference and Deduction Skills for Reading: Literature Review.* London: DCSF.

Lauchlan, F. (2012) Bilingualism in Sardinia and Scotland: exploring the cognitive benefits of speaking a 'minority' language. *International Journal of Bilingualism,* 16: 3.

Lazar, R., Warr-Leeper, G., Nicholson, C. and Johnson, S. (1989) Elementary school teachers' use of multiple meaning expressions. *Language, Speech and Hearing Services in Schools,* 20: 420–430.

Lee, W. (2011) *Talk Boost Interim Report.* London: ICAN.

Lindsay, G., Dockrell, J., Law, J. and Roulstone, S. (2011) *Better Communication Research Programme: 2nd Interim Report.* London: DfE.

Locke, A., Ginsborg, J. and Peers, I. (2002) Development and disadvantage: implications for early years and beyond. *International Journal of Language and Communication Disorders*, 37(1): 3–15.

McCartney, E., Boyle, J., Ellis, S., Bannatyne, S. and Turnbull, M. (2011) Indirect language therapy for children with persistent language impairment in mainstream primary schools: outcomes from a cohort intervention. *International Journal of Language and Communication Disorders*, 46(1): 74–82.

Moseley, D., Clark, J., Baumfield, V., Hall, E., Hall, I., Miller, J., Blench, G., Gregson, M. and Spedding, T. (2006) *The Impact of ESB Oral Communication Courses in HM Prisons: An Independent Evaluation*. London: Learning and Skills Development Agency.

Nagy, W., Anderson, R. and Herman, P. (1987) Learning word meanings from normal reading. *American Educational Research Journal*, 24: 237–270.

Nash, H. and Snowling, M. (2006) Teaching new words to children with poor existing vocabulary knowledge. *International Journal of Language and Communication Disorders*, 41: 335–354.

National Literacy Trust (2010) *Highlights from a Literature Review Prepared for the Face to Face Research Project*. London: National Literacy Trust.

National Literacy Trust (2011) *2011 Schools Guide*. London: National Literacy Trust.

Ofsted (2011a) *Developing the Indoor and Outdoor Environments to Support and Promote Children's Communication Skills: Townsend Children's Centre*. London: Ofsted.

Ofsted (2011b) *Excellence in English*. London: Ofsted.

Ofsted (2012) *The Framework for School Inspection*. London: Ofsted.

Organisation for Economic Co-operation and Development (2012) *PISA: Let's Read Them a Story! The Parent Factor in Education*. Paris: OECD.

Pan, B., Rowe, M., Singer, J. and Snow, C. (2005) Maternal correlates of growth in toddler vocabulary production in low income families. *Child Development*, 76: 763–782.

Parsons, S. and Branagan, A. (2013) *Word Aware: A Whole School Approach for Developing Spoken and Written Vocabulary*. Milton Keynes: Speechmark.

Ripley, K. and Barratt, J. (2008) *Supporting Speech, Language and Communication Needs*. London: Sage.

Roulstone, S., Law, J., Rush, R., Clegg, J. and Peters, T. (2011) *Investigating the Role of Language in Children's Early Educational Outcomes*. London: DfE.

Scott, J. A., Jamieson-Noel, D. and Asselin, M. (2003) Vocabulary instruction throughout the day in 23 Canadian upper-elementary classrooms. *Elementary School Journal*, 103: 269–286.

Scottish Social Research Executive (2005) *Literature of the NEET Group*. Edinburgh: Scottish Social Research Executive.

Siraj-Blatchford, I., Shepherd, D., Melhuish E., Taggart, B., Sammons, P. and Sylva, K. (2011) *Effective Primary Pedagogical Strategies in English and Mathematics*. London: DfE.

Snowling, M. (2006) Language skills and learning to read: the dyslexia spectrum. In M. Snowling and R. Stackhouse (eds), *Dyslexia, Speech and Language: A Practitioners' Handbook*, 1–14. Chichester: John Wiley.

Snowling, M., Clarke, P. and Hulme, C. (2010) *Reading Comprehension: Nature, Assessment and Teaching*. London: Economic and Social Research Council.

Spencer, S., Clegg, J. and Stackhouse, J. (2012) Language and disadvantage: a comparison of the language abilities of adolescents from two different socio-economic areas. *International Journal of Language and Communication Disorders*, 47: 3.

Spooner, L. and Woodcock, J. (2010) *Teaching Children to Listen*. London: Continuum Press.

Stahl, S. and Nagy, W. (2006) *Teaching Word Meanings*. Mahwah, NJ: Lawrence Erlbaum.

Starling, J. (2011) Creating 'language-accessible' secondary school classrooms through professional collaborations. Presentation at 'Lost for Words: Lost for Life?', conference at City University, London, 15–17 June.

Steele, S. and Mills, M. (2011) Vocabulary intervention for school aged children with language impairment: a review of the evidence and good practice. *Child Language Teaching and Therapy*, 27(3): 354–70.

UK Commission for Employment and Skills (2010) *The Employability Challenge*. Wath upon Dearne: UK Commission for Employment and Skills. Available at www.ukces.org.uk/tags/employability-challenge-full-report.

Waldfogel, J. and Washbrook, E. (2010) *Low Income and Early Cognitive Development in the UK*. London: Sutton Trust.

White, H. and Evans, C. (2005) *Learning to Listen to Learn: Using Multi-Sensory Teaching for Effective Listening*. London: Sage.

Wolf, M. (2007) *Proust and the Squid*. New York: HarperCollins.

Index